T0088527

Cover photo: Photofest

ISBN 978-1-4234-8921-4

Exclusively Distributed By

HAL•LEONARD®
CORPORATION
7777 W. BLUEMOUND RD. P.O. BOX 13819 MILWAUKEE, WI 53213

For all works contained herein:
Unauthorized copying, arranging, adapting, recording, Internet posting, public performance,
or other distribution of the printed music in this publication is an infringement of copyright.
Infringers are liable under the law.

Visit Hal Leonard Online at
www.halleonard.com

STRUM AND PICK PATTERNS

This chart contains the suggested strum and pick patterns that are referred to by number at the beginning of each song in this book. The symbols ⊓ and ∨ in the strum patterns refer to down and up strokes, respectively. The letters in the pick patterns indicate which right-hand fingers play which strings.

p = thumb
i = index finger
m = middle finger
a = ring finger

For example; Pick Pattern 2
is played: thumb - index - middle - ring

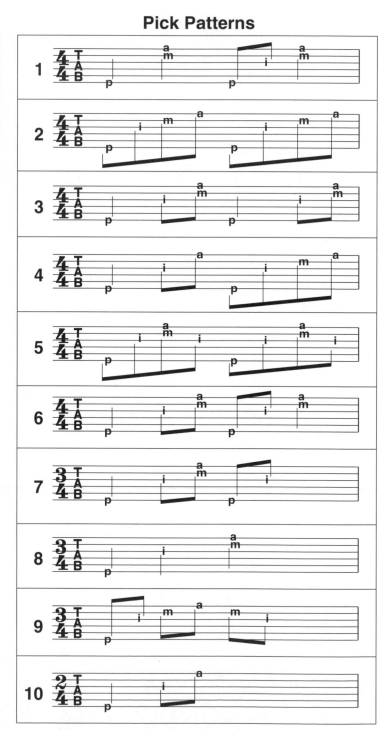

You can use the 3/4 Strum and Pick Patterns in songs written in compound meter (6/8, 9/8, 12/8, etc.). For example, you can accompany a song in 6/8 by playing the 3/4 pattern twice in each measure. The 4/4 Strum and Pick Patterns can be used for songs written in cut time (¢) by doubling the note time values in the patterns. Each pattern would therefore last two measures in cut time.

GUITAR NOTATION LEGEND

Guitar music can be notated three different ways: on a *musical staff*, in *tablature*, and in *rhythm slashes*.

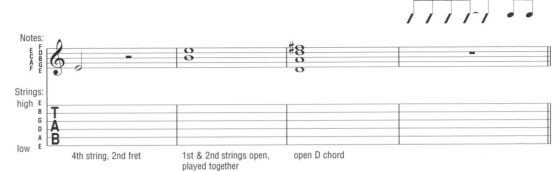

RHYTHM SLASHES are written above the staff. Strum chords in the rhythm indicated. Use the chord diagrams found at the top of the first page of the transcription for the appropriate chord voicings. Round noteheads indicate single notes.

THE MUSICAL STAFF shows pitches and rhythms and is divided by bar lines into measures. Pitches are named after the first seven letters of the alphabet.

TABLATURE graphically represents the guitar fingerboard. Each horizontal line represents a string, and each number represents a fret.

HALF-STEP BEND: Strike the note and bend up 1/2 step.

WHOLE-STEP BEND: Strike the note and bend up one step.

GRACE NOTE BEND: Strike the note and immediately bend up as indicated.

SLIGHT (MICROTONE) BEND: Strike the note and bend up 1/4 step.

BEND AND RELEASE: Strike the note and bend up as indicated, then release back to the original note. Only the first note is struck.

PRE-BEND: Bend the note as indicated, then strike it.

VIBRATO: The string is vibrated by rapidly bending and releasing the note with the fretting hand.

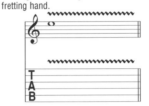

WIDE VIBRATO: The pitch is varied to a greater degree by vibrating with the fretting hand.

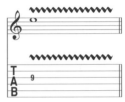

HAMMER-ON: Strike the first (lower) note with one finger, then sound the higher note (on the same string) with another finger by fretting it without picking.

PULL-OFF: Place both fingers on the notes to be sounded. Strike the first note and without picking, pull the finger off to sound the second (lower) note.

LEGATO SLIDE: Strike the first note and then slide the same fret-hand finger up or down to the second note. The second note is not struck.

SHIFT SLIDE: Same as legato slide, except the second note is struck.

TRILL: Very rapidly alternate between the notes indicated by continuously hammering on and pulling off.

TAPPING: Hammer ("tap") the fret indicated with the pick-hand index or middle finger and pull off to the note fretted by the fret hand.

NATURAL HARMONIC: Strike the note while the fret-hand lightly touches the string directly over the fret indicated.

PINCH HARMONIC: The note is fretted normally and a harmonic is produced by adding the edge of the thumb or the tip of the index finger of the pick hand to the normal pick attack.

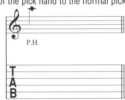

PICK SCRAPE: The edge of the pick is rubbed down (or up) the string, producing a scratchy sound.

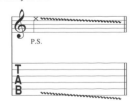

MUFFLED STRINGS: A percussive sound is produced by laying the fret hand across the string(s) without depressing, and striking them with the pick hand.

PALM MUTING: The note is partially muted by the pick hand lightly touching the string(s) just before the bridge.

RAKE: Drag the pick across the strings indicated with a single motion.

TREMOLO PICKING: The note is picked as rapidly and continuously as possible.

VIBRATO BAR DIVE AND RETURN: The pitch of the note or chord is dropped a specified number of steps (in rhythm), then returned to the original pitch.

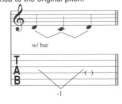

VIBRATO BAR SCOOP: Depress the bar just before striking the note, then quickly release the bar.

VIBRATO BAR DIP: Strike the note and then immediately drop a specified number of steps, then release back to the original pitch.

Back in Black

Words and Music by Angus Young, Malcolm Young and Brian Johnson

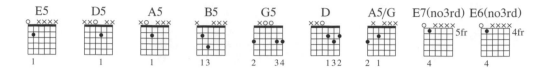

E5   D5   A5   B5   G5   D   A5/G   E7(no3rd)   E6(no3rd)

Strum Pattern: 3
Pick Pattern: 3

Intro
Moderately slow Rock

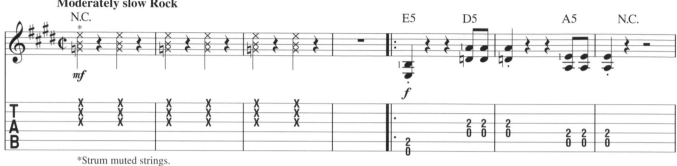

*Strum muted strings.

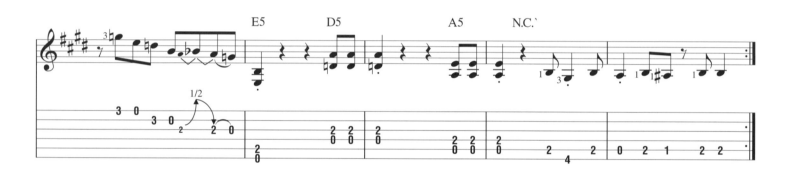

Verse
w/ Intro rhythm

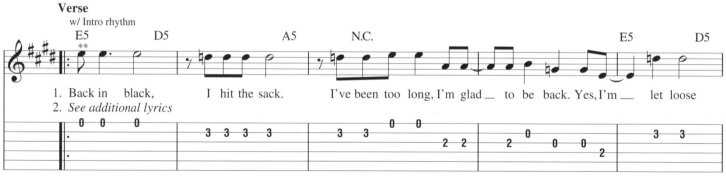

1. Back in black, I hit the sack. I've been too long, I'm glad __ to be back. Yes, I'm __ let loose
2. *See additional lyrics*

**Sung one octave higher throughout.

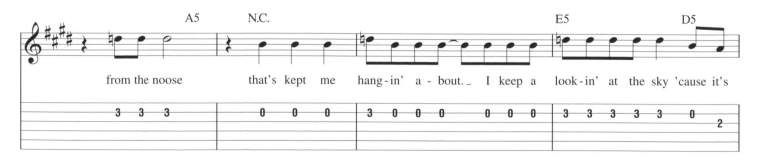

from the noose that's kept me hang-in' a-bout. __ I keep a look-in' at the sky 'cause it's

Copyright © 1980 J. Albert & Son Pty., Ltd.
International Copyright Secured   All Rights Reserved

get-tin' me high. For-get the hearse 'cause I'll nev-er die. I got nine lives, cat's eyes. A-

% Chorus

bus-in' ev-'ry one of them and run-nin' wild. 'Cause I'm back. Yes, I'm back.

*Optional: Use 3rd finger on A5.

Well, I'm back. Yes, I'm ___ back. Well, I'm back, ___

To Coda ⊕

back. ___ Well, I'm back in black. Yes, I'm back in ___ black. ___ Oh!

Guitar Solo

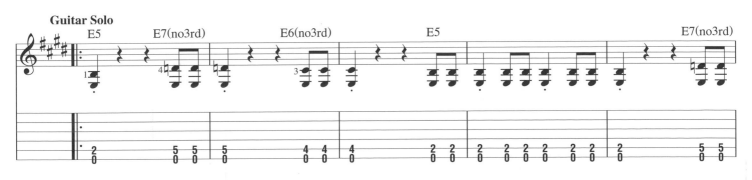

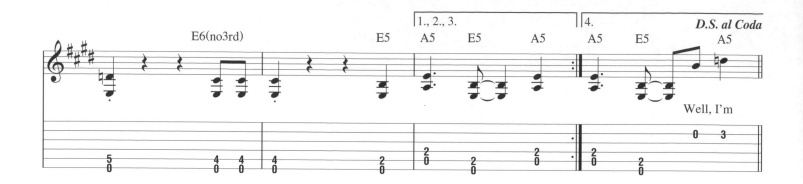

*Chords in parentheses reflect implied harmony.

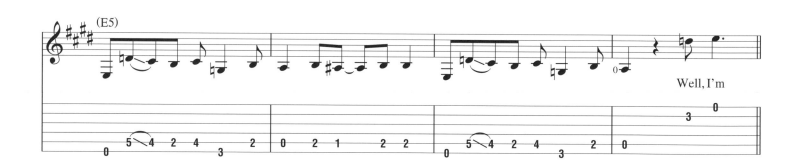

Well, I'm

back, _____ back. _____ Well, I'm back, _____

**Rhythm as before.

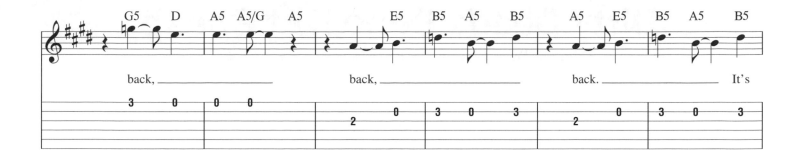

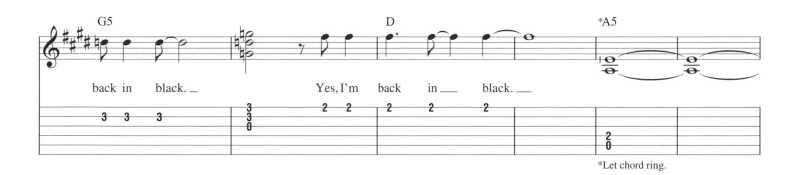

*Let chord ring.

Outro-Guitar Solo

Repeat and fade

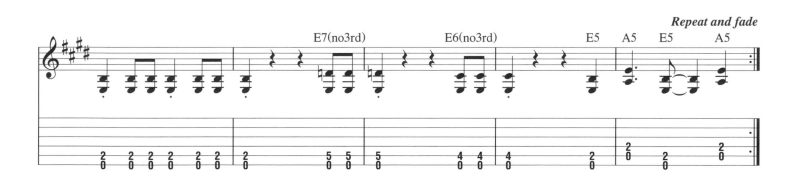

Additional Lyrics

2. Back in the back of a Cadillac.
Number one with a bullet, I'm a power pack.
Yes, I'm in the band, with the gang.
They got to catch me if they want me to hang
'Cause I'm back on the track, and I'm beatin' the flack.
Nobody's gonna get me on another rap.
So look at me now, I'm just a makin' my play.
Don't try to push your luck, just get outta my way.

Dirty Deeds Done Dirt Cheap

Words and Music by Angus Young, Malcolm Young and Bon Scott

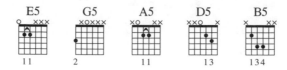

Strum Pattern: 1
Pick Pattern: 1

Intro

Moderate Rock

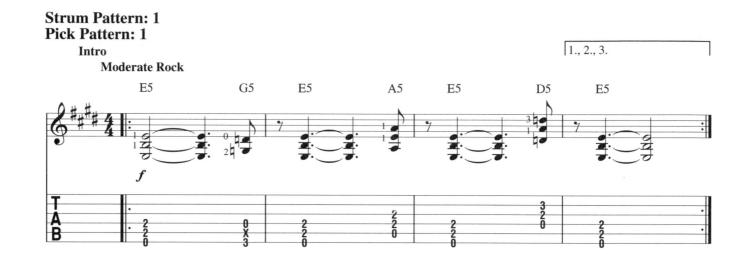

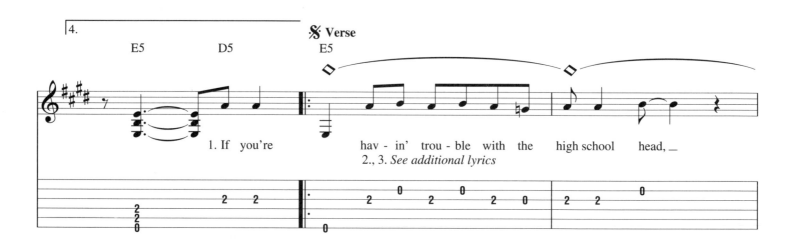

1. If you're hav - in' trou - ble with the high school head, ⸺
2., 3. *See additional lyrics*

he's giv - in' you the blues. ⸺⸺ You wan - na grad - u - ate but

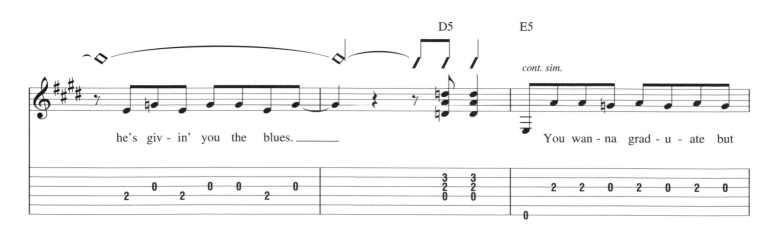

Copyright © 1976 by J. Albert & Son Pty., Ltd.
International Copyright Secured   All Rights Reserved

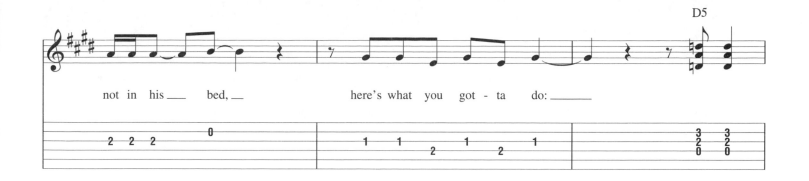

not in his ___ bed, ___ here's what you got - ta do: _____

pick up the phone, I'm ___ al - ways home. Call me an - y - time. ___ Just ring

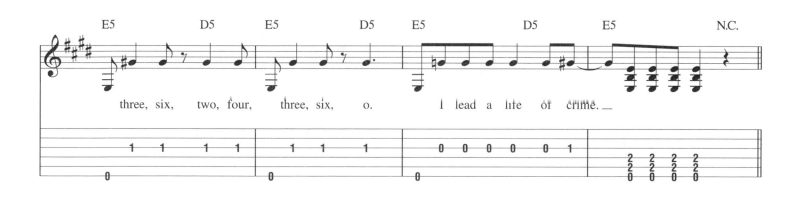

three, six, two, four, three, six, o. I lead a life of crime. _

Chorus

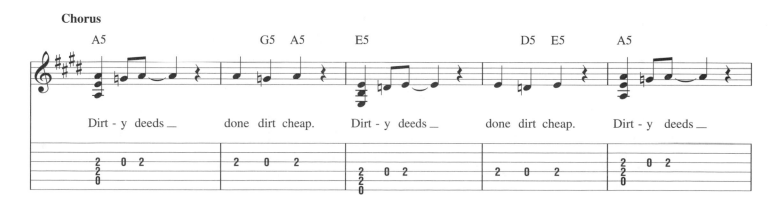

Dirt - y deeds ___ done dirt cheap. Dirt - y deeds ___ done dirt cheap. Dirt - y deeds ___

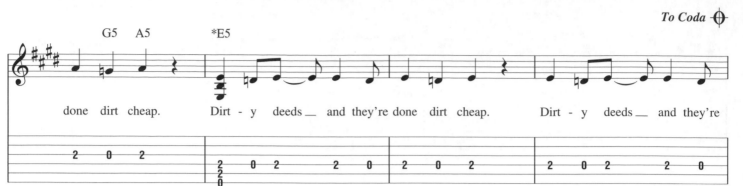

done dirt cheap.   Dirt - y deeds __ and they're done dirt cheap.   Dirt - y deeds __ and they're

*Let chord ring.

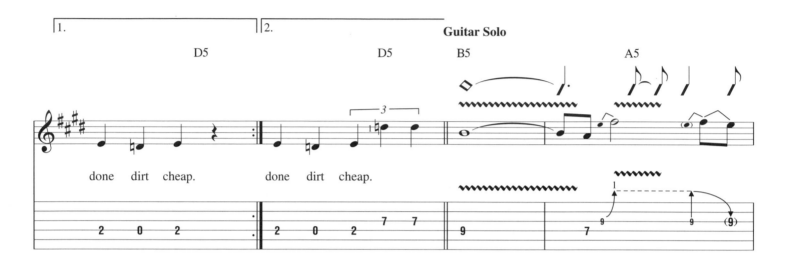

done   dirt cheap.   done   dirt cheap.

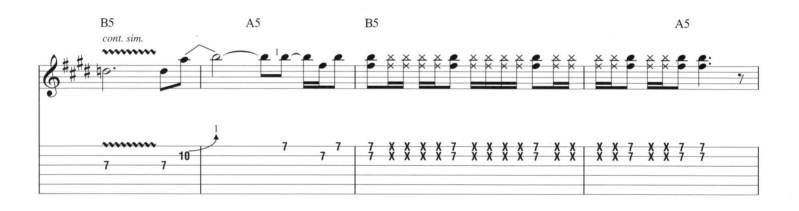

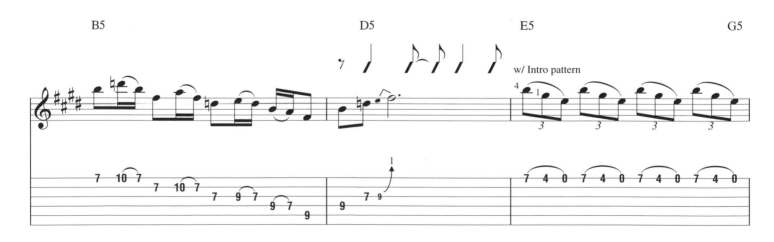

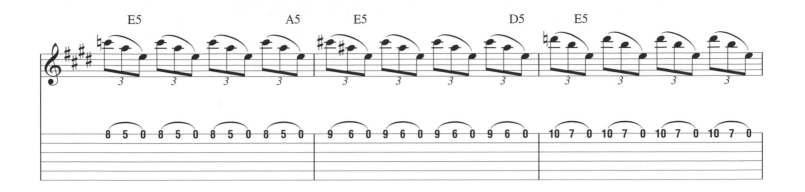

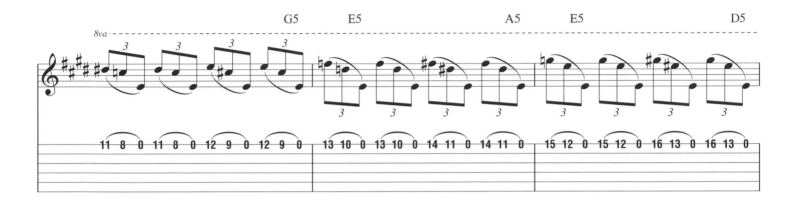

D.S. al Coda ⊕ **Coda**

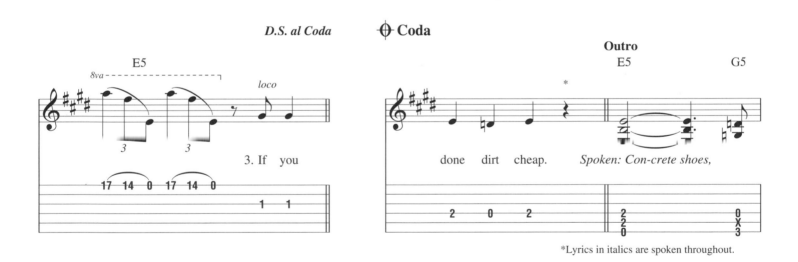

3. If you

done dirt cheap. *Spoken: Con-crete shoes,*

Outro

*Lyrics in italics are spoken throughout.

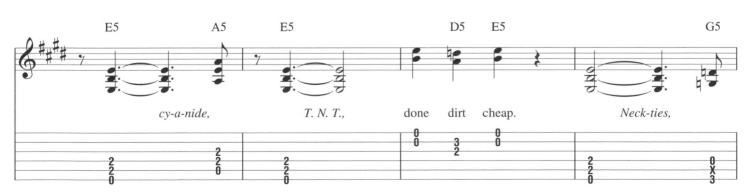

cy-a-nide,   *T. N. T.,*   done dirt cheap.   *Neck-ties,*

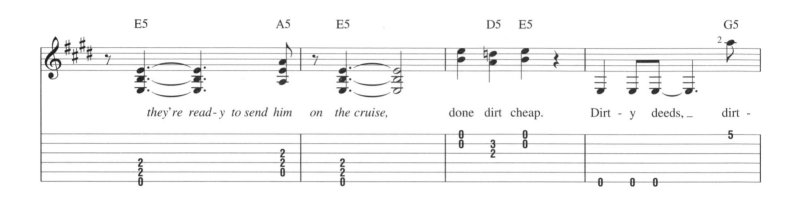

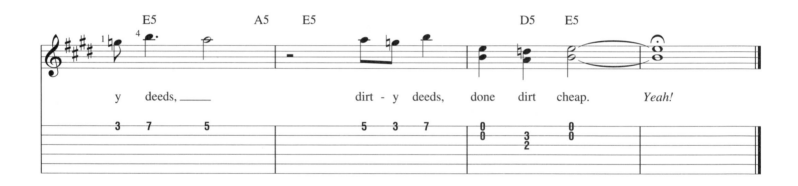

Additional Lyrics

2. You got problems in your life of love,
   You got a broken heart.
   He's double-dealin' with your best friend,
   That's when the teardrops start, fella.
   Pick up the phone, I'm here alone,
   Or make a social call.
   Come right in, forget about him,
   We'll have ourselves a ball.

3. If you got a lady and you want her gone,
   But you ain't got the guts.
   She keeps naggin' at you night and day,
   Enough to drive you nuts.
   Pick up the phone, leave her alone,
   It's time you made a stand.
   For a fee, I'm happy to be
   Your back door man. Whoo!

For Those About to Rock
(We Salute You)

Words and Music by Angus Young, Malcolm Young and Brian Johnson

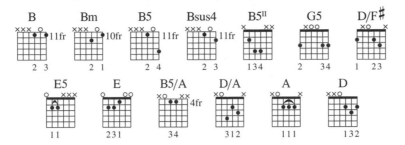

Strum Pattern: 3, 6
Pick Pattern: 1

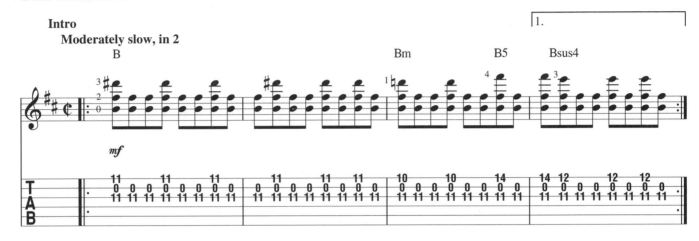

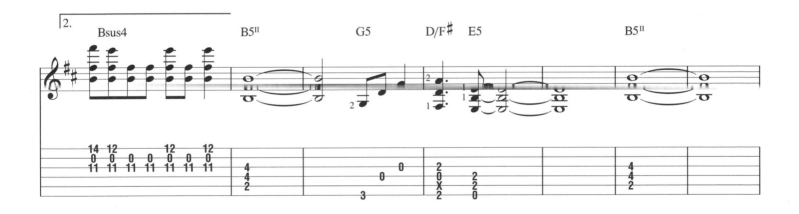

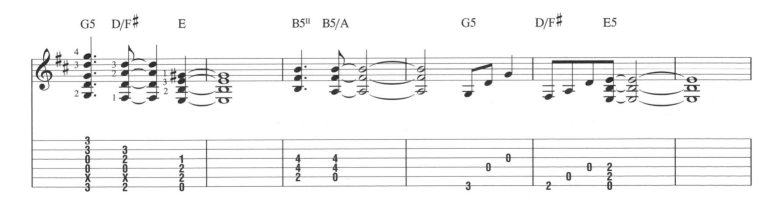

Copyright © 1981 by J. Albert & Son Pty., Ltd.
International Copyright Secured   All Rights Reserved

Spoken: Oh!

*Lyrics in italics are spoken throughout.

Chorus

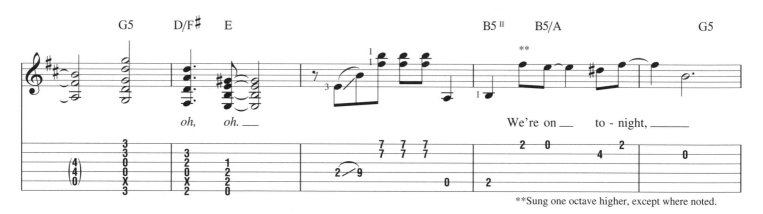

Yeah, yeah, ___ yeah, yeah, ___

oh, oh. ___ We're on ___ to - night, _____

**Sung one octave higher, except where noted.

to the gui - tar bite. ___ Yeah, yeah, _____ oh. ___

Verse

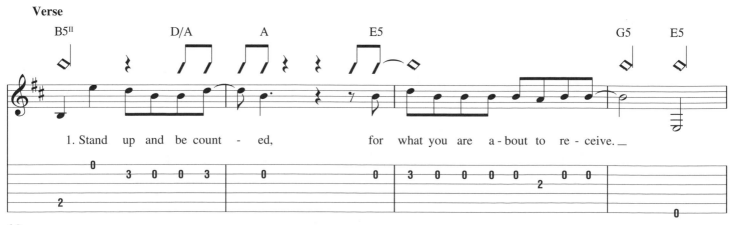

1. Stand up and be count - ed, for what you are a - bout to re - ceive. ___

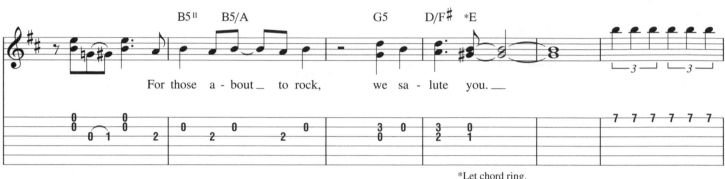

*Let chord ring.

Guitar Solo

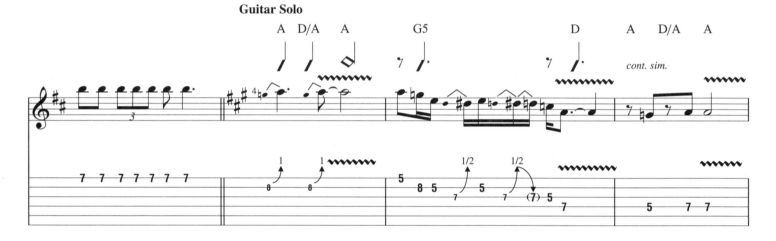

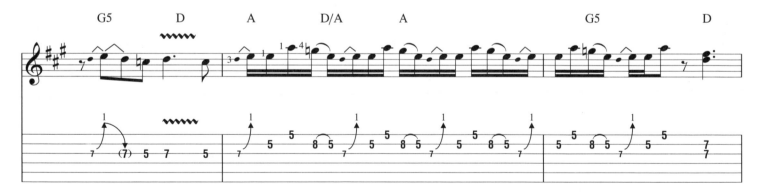

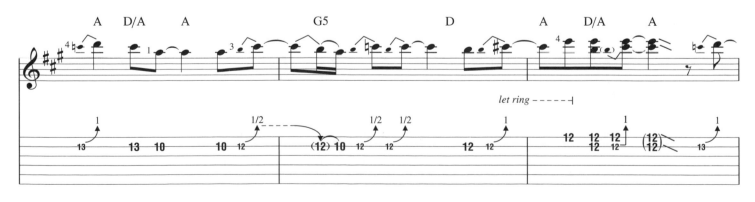

D.S. al Coda

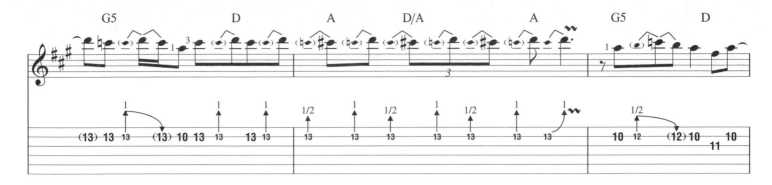

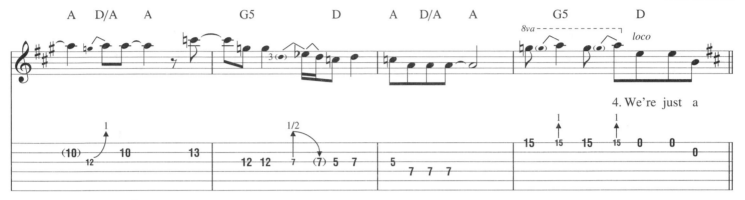

*Background vocals sung as written.

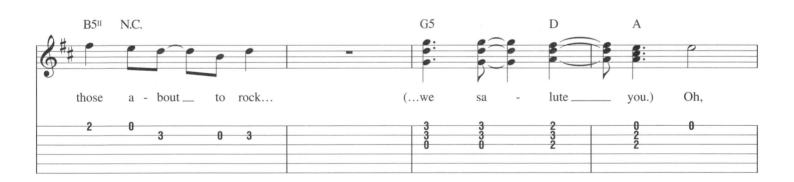

19

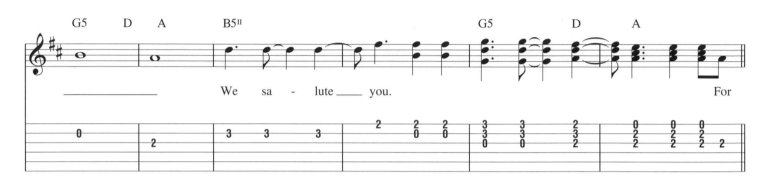

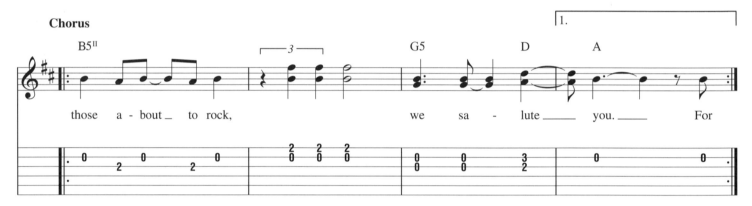

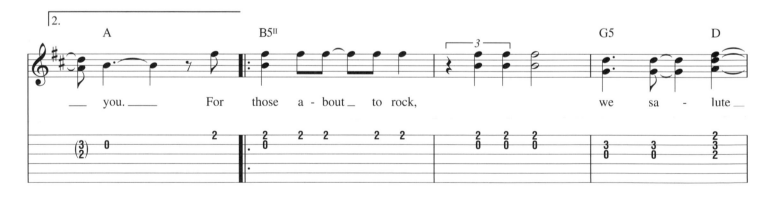

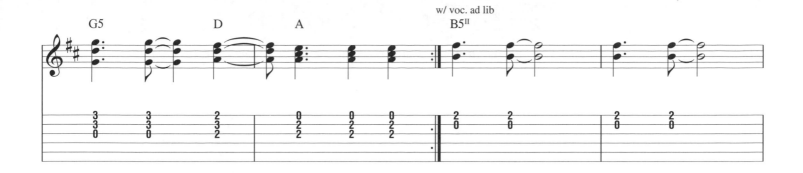

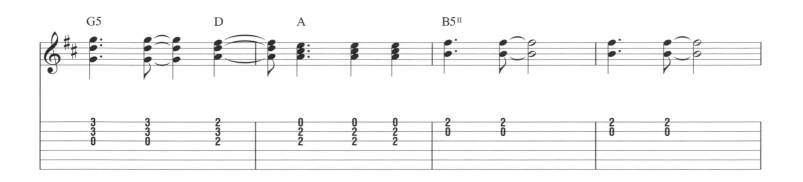

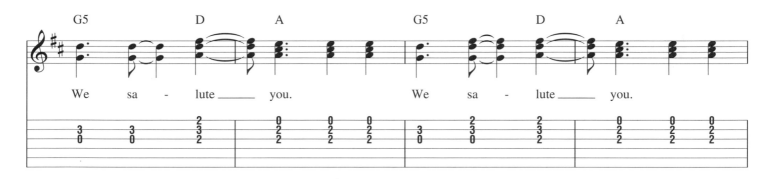

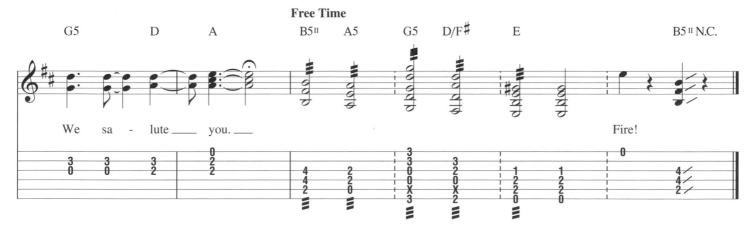

Additional Lyrics

3. We rock at dawn on the front line,
   Like a bolt right out of the blue.
   The sky's alight with the guitar bite.
   Heads will roll and rock tonight.

4. We're just a battery for hire with a guitar fire,
   Ready and aimed at you.
   Pick up your balls, and load up your cannon
   For a twenty-one gun salute.

Girls Got Rhythm

Words and Music by Angus Young, Malcolm Young and Bon Scott

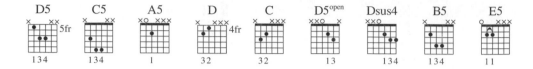

Strum Pattern: 1, 6

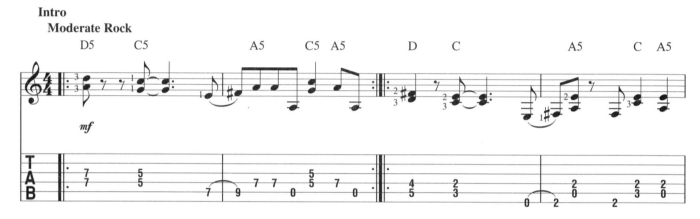

*Sung one octave higher throughout.

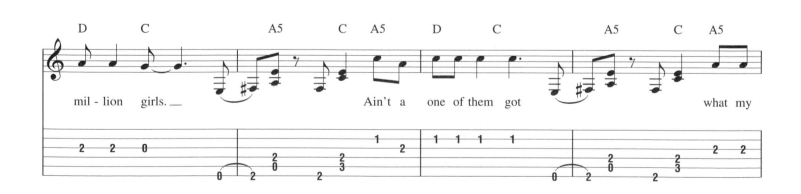

Copyright © 1979 by J. Albert & Son Pty., Ltd.
International Copyright Secured   All Rights Reserved

la - dy she's got. __ She's steal - ing the spot - light, knocks me

off my feet. __ She's e - nough to start a land - slide, just a

𝄋 Pre-Chorus

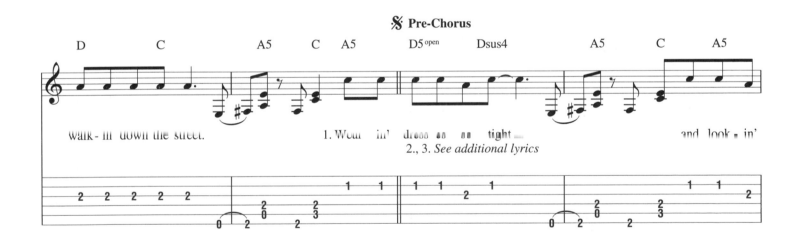

walk - in' down the street. 1. Wear - in' dress - es so tight __ and look - in'

2., 3. *See additional lyrics*

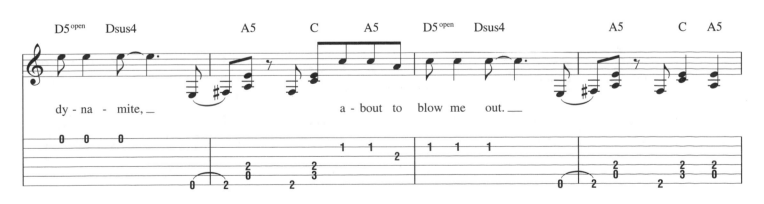

dy - na - mite, __ a - bout to blow me out. __

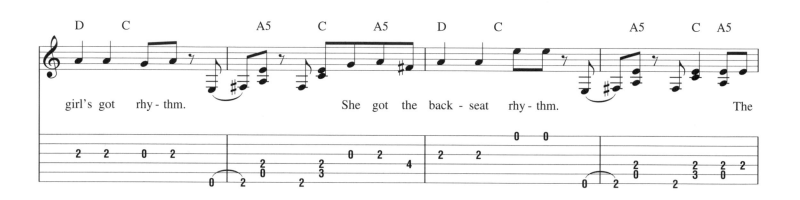

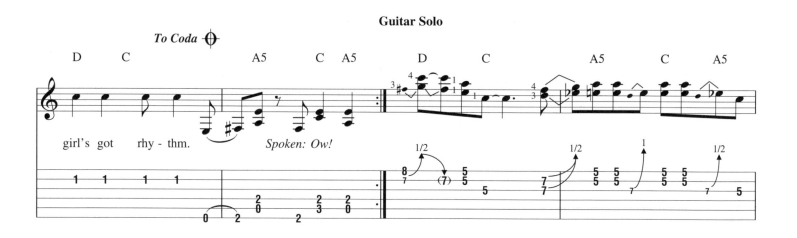

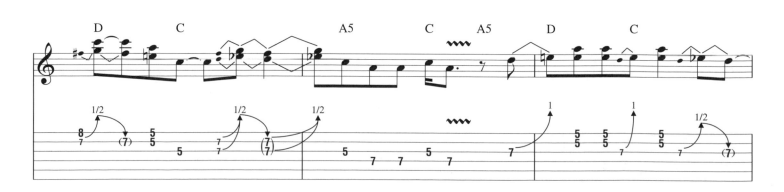

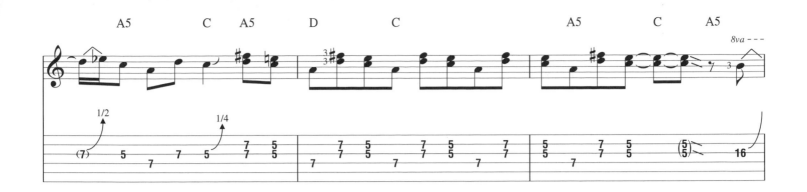

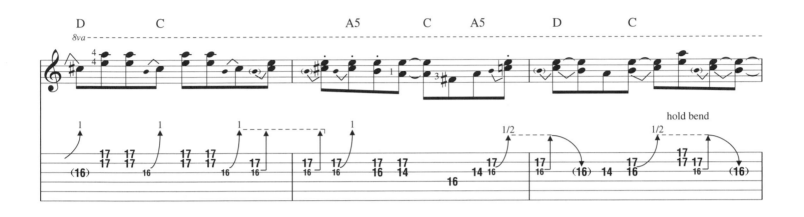

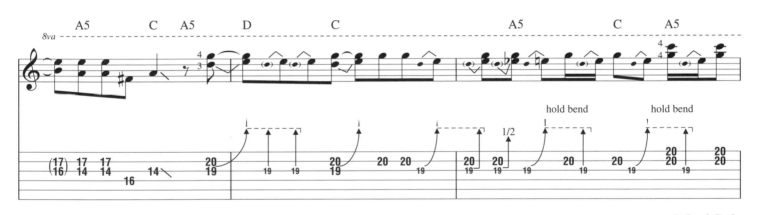

D.S. al Coda

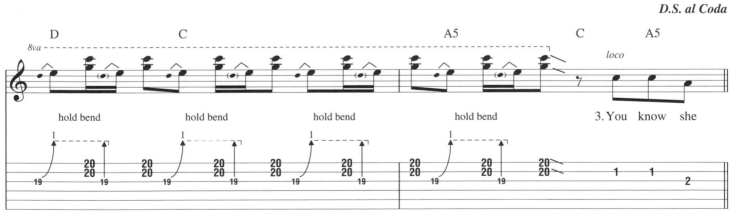

⊕ Coda

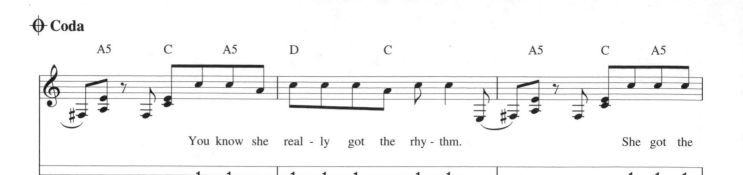

You know she real-ly got the rhy-thm. She got the

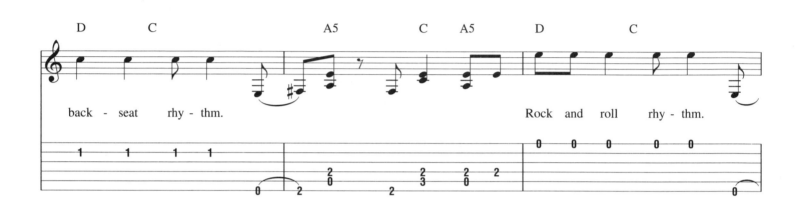

back - seat rhy-thm. Rock and roll rhy-thm.

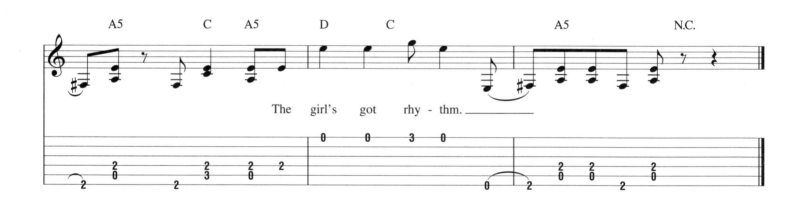

The girl's got rhy-thm. _____

Additional Lyrics

2. She's like a lethal brand, too much for any man.
   She give me first degree, she really satisfy me.
   Love me till I'm legless, achin' and sore.
   Enough to stop a freight train or start the third world war.

Pre-Chorus 2. You know I'm losin' sleep, but I'm in too deep.
   Like a body need blood,
   No doubt about it, can't live without it.

Pre-Chorus 3. You know she moves like sin, and when she let me in,
   It's like liquid love.
   No doubt about it, can't live without it.

Moneytalks

Words and Music by Angus Young and Malcolm Young

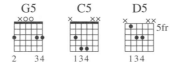

Strum Pattern: 2, 6
Pick Pattern: 4

Intro
Moderate Rock

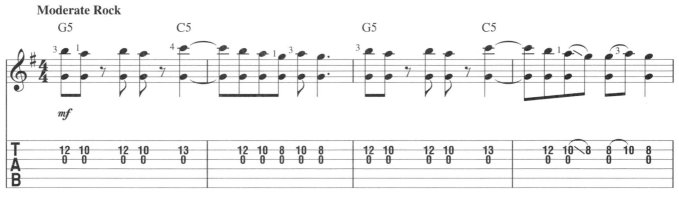

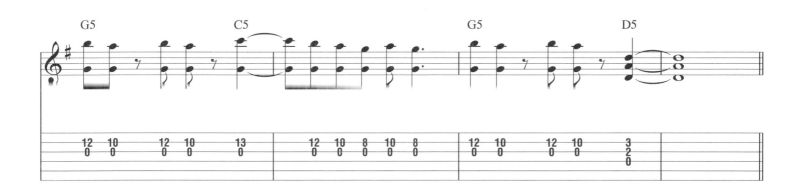

*Sung one octave
higher throughout.

Copyright © 1990 by J. Albert & Son Pty., Ltd.
International Copyright Secured   All Rights Reserved

Verse

suits, chauf - feured cars, fine ho - tels, and big ci - gars up for
2. See additional lyrics

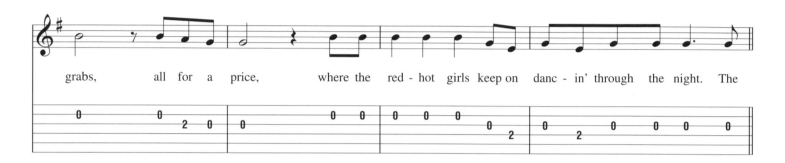

grabs, all for a price, where the red - hot girls keep on danc - in' through the night. The

Pre-Chorus

claim is on __ you, __ the sights are on __ me, __ so what do you do _____ that's __
See additional lyrics

__ guar - an - teed? __ Hey, __ lit - tle girl, you want it all: the

𝄋 Chorus

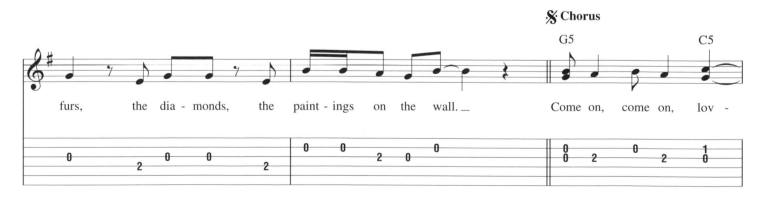

furs, the dia - monds, the paint - ings on the wall. __ Come on, come on, lov -

28

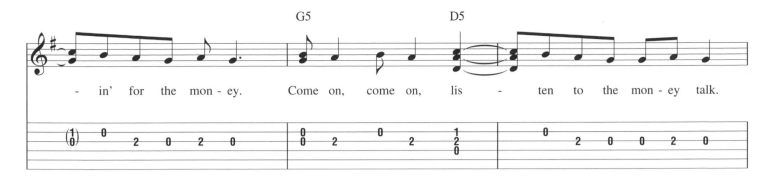

-in' for the mon-ey. Come on, come on, lis - ten to the mon-ey talk.

3rd time, To Coda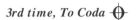

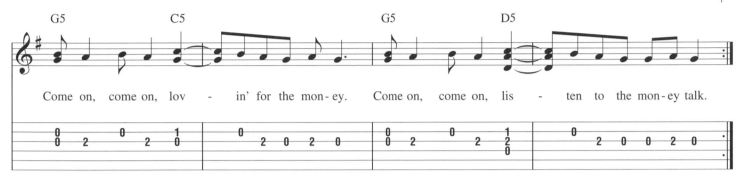

Come on, come on, lov - in' for the mon-ey. Come on, come on, lis - ten to the mon-ey talk.

Interlude

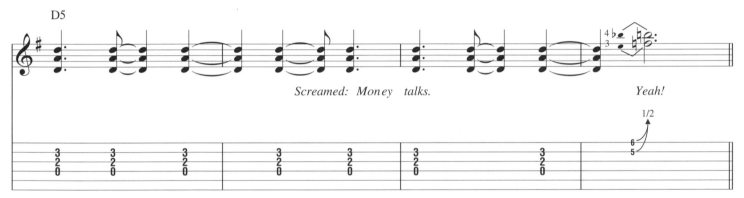

Screamed: Money talks.   *Yeah!*

Guitar Solo

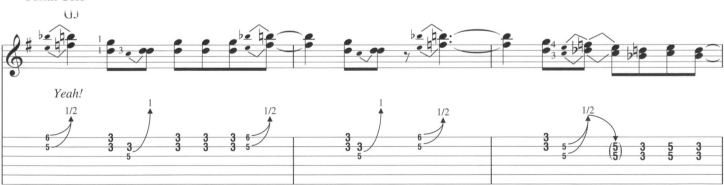

Yeah!

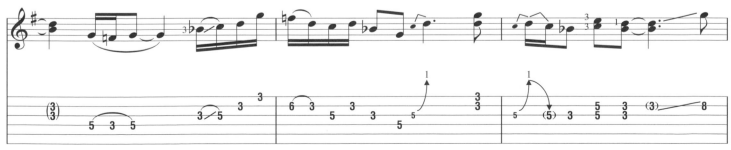

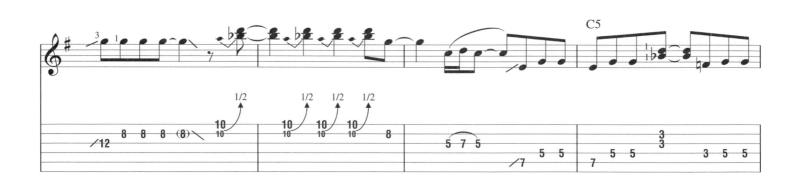

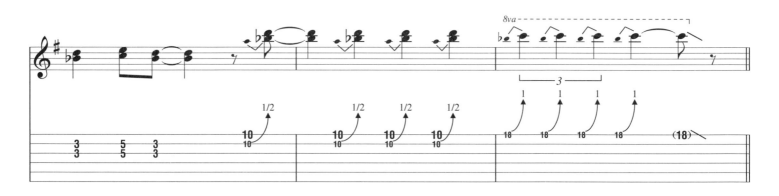

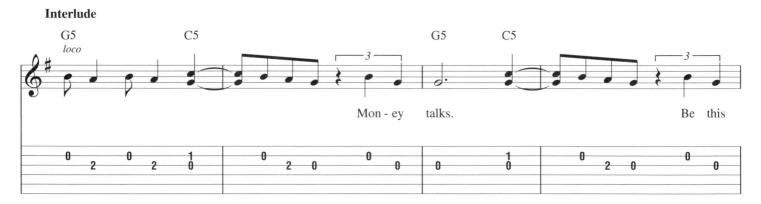

Interlude

Mon - ey talks.

Be this

D.S. al Coda

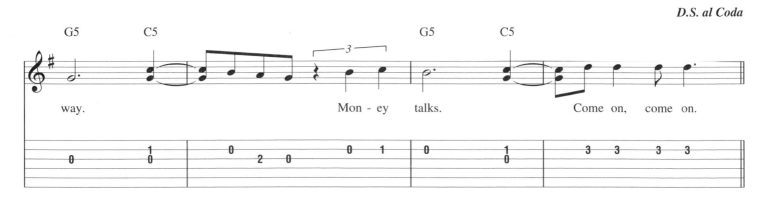

way.

Mon - ey talks.

Come on, come on.

Coda

w/ Lead Voc. ad lib.

(Come one, come on, lov - in' for the mon - ey. Come on, come on, lis -

*Background vocals sung as written.

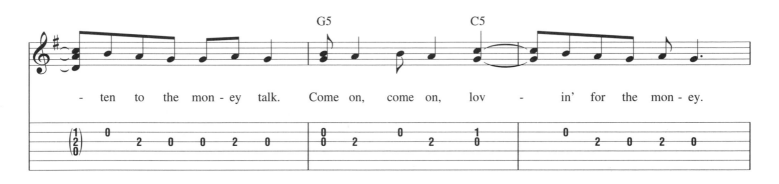

- ten to the mon - ey talk. Come on, come on, lov - in' for the mon - ey.

Outro

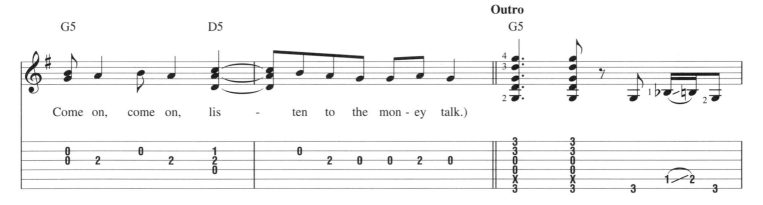

Come on, come on, lis - ten to the mon - ey talk.)

Additional Lyrics

2. A French maid, foreign chef,
   A big house with king-size beds.
   You had enough, you ship 'em out.
   The dollar's up, down, you better buy the pound.

Pre-Chorus The claim is on you, the sights are on me,
   So what do you do that's guaranteed?
   Hey little girl, you break the laws,
   You hustle, you deal, you steal from us all.

Have a Drink on Me

Words and Music by Angus Young, Malcolm Young and Brian Johnson

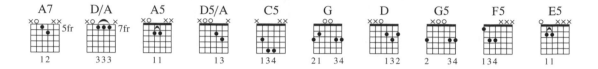

Strum Pattern: 1, 6
Pick Pattern: 1, 3

Intro
Moderate Rock

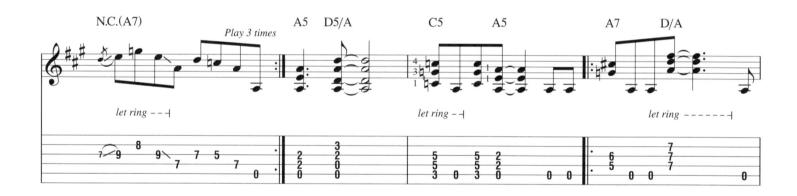

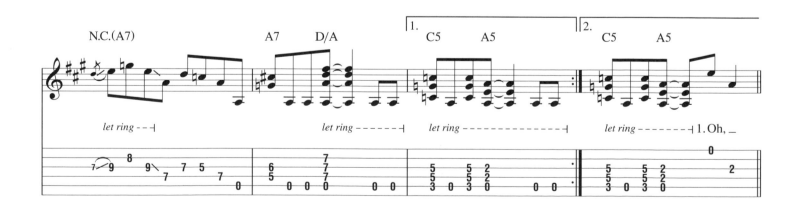

Copyright © 1980 by J. Albert & Son Pty., Ltd.
International Copyright Secured   All Rights Reserved

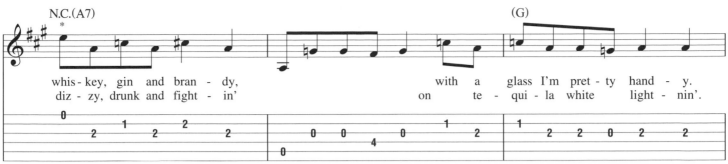

*Sung one octave higher throughout.

whis - key, gin and bran - dy,
diz - zy, drunk and fight - in'

with a glass I'm pret - ty hand - y.
on te - qui - la white light - nin'.

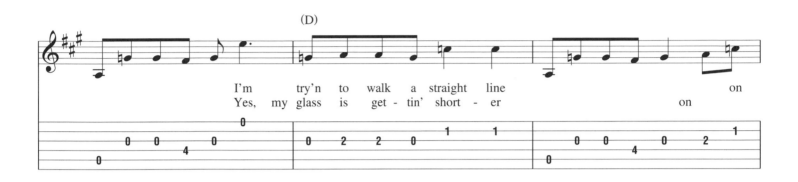

I'm try'n to walk a straight line
Yes, my glass is get - tin' short - er

on

on

sour ___ mash and cheap wine.
whis - key, ice and wa - ter.

Yeah, so join me for a drink, boys,
Yeah, so come on, have a good time,

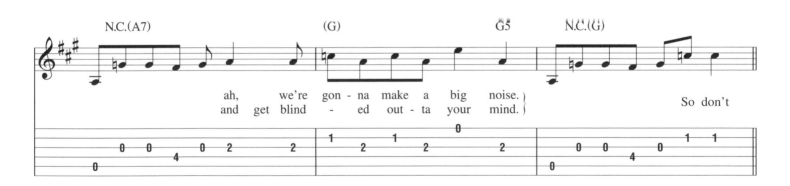

ah, we're gon - na make a big noise. }
and get blind - ed out - ta your mind. }

So don't

Pre-Chorus

wor - ry 'bout to - mor - row,
take it to - day. ___
For - get a - bout the check, we'll get

Chorus

hell   to   pay.___   Oh, have a   drink on ___ me.___   Yeah, have   a

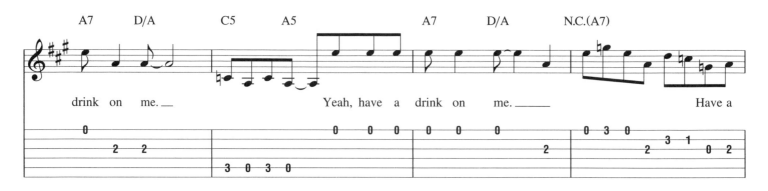

drink   on   me.___   Yeah, have   a   drink   on   me._____   Have a

To Coda ⊕

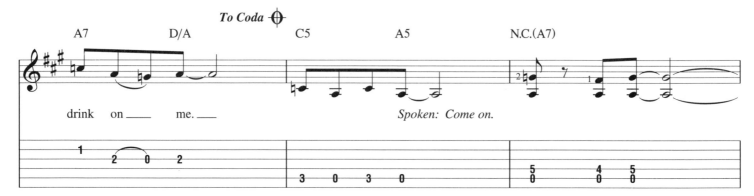

drink   on ___   me. ___   *Spoken: Come on.*

D.S. al Coda

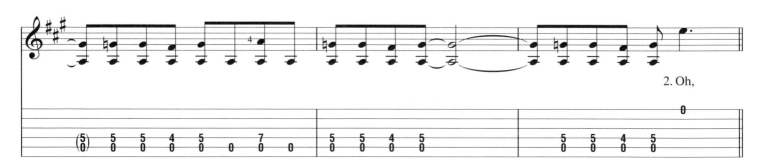

2. Oh,

⊕ **Coda**

Guitar Solo

Get stoned!

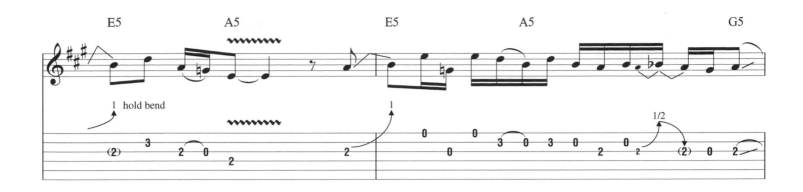

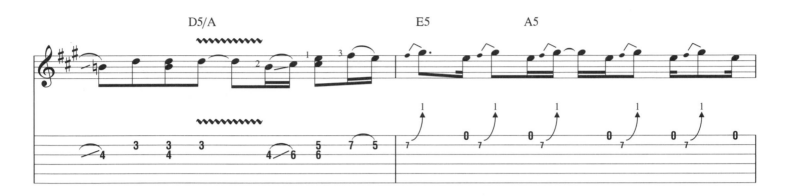

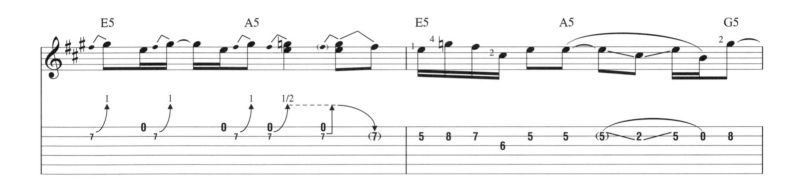

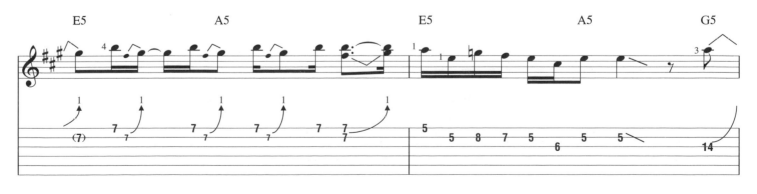

Chorus

Have a drink on me. _____ Oh, have a

drink on me, __ yeah! __ Oh, have a drink on me. __ Come on!

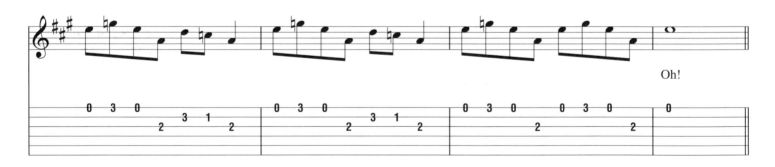

Oh!

Bridge

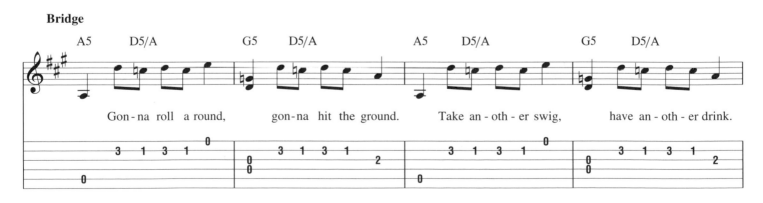

Gon-na roll a round, gon-na hit the ground. Take an-oth-er swig, have an-oth-er drink.

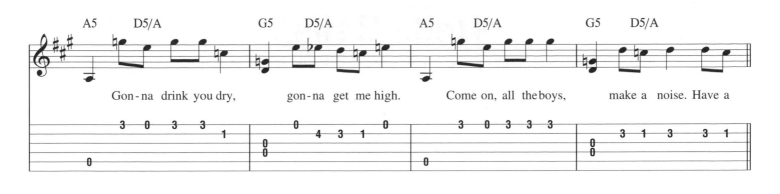

Gon-na drink you dry, gon-na get me high. Come on, all the boys, make a noise. Have a

Outro-Chorus

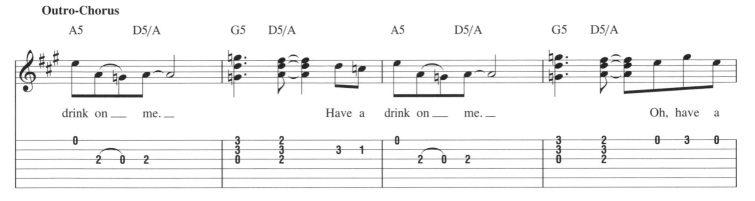

drink on ___ me. ___ Have a drink on ___ me. ___ Oh, have a

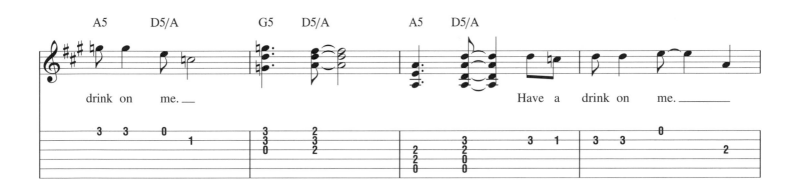

drink on me. ___ Have a drink on me. _____

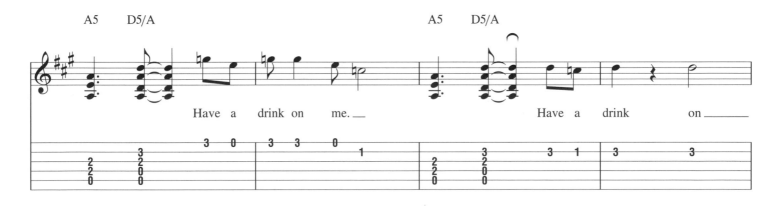

Have a drink on me. ___ Have a drink on _____

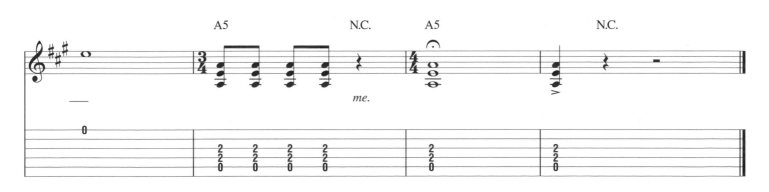

___ me.

Hells Bells

Words and Music by Angus Young, Malcolm Young and Brian Johnson

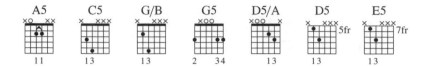

Strum Pattern: 1, 3
Pick Pattern: 1, 3

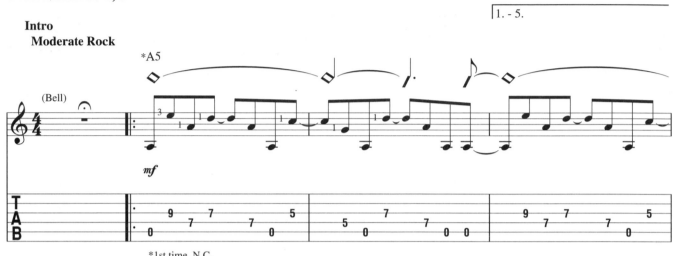

*1st time, N.C.
5th time, cont. in notation

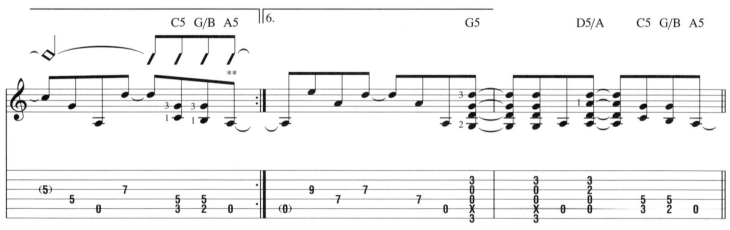

**Tie into beat 1 on repeat.

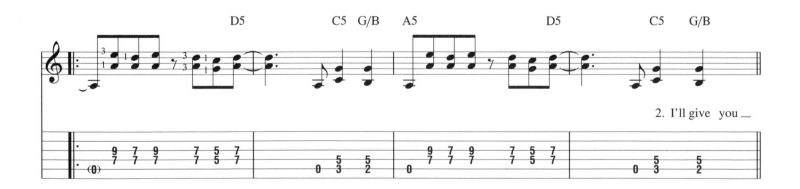

Copyright © 1980 by J. Albert & Son Pty., Ltd.
International Copyright Secured   All Rights Reserved

Verse

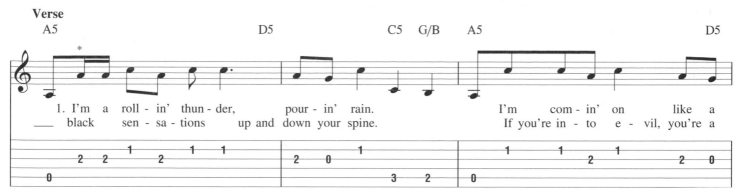

*Sung one octave higher throughout.

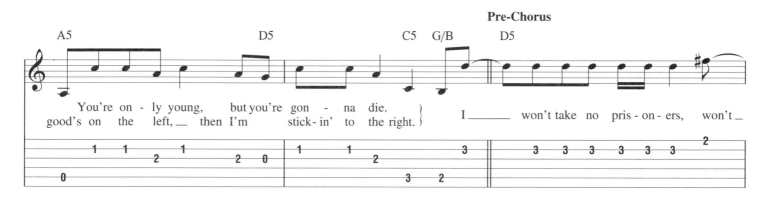

Pre-Chorus

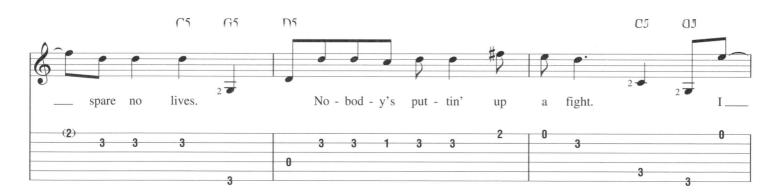

Chorus

bells. __ (Yeah,/Oh,) hell's bells. __ You got me ring-in' hell's

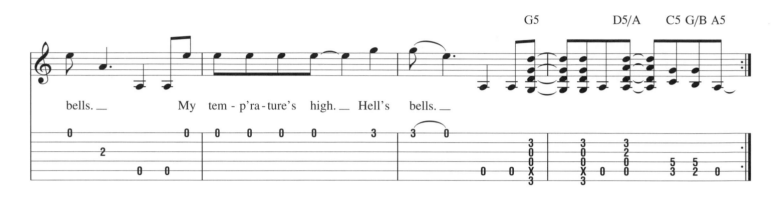

bells. __ My tem-p'ra-ture's high. __ Hell's bells. __

Guitar Solo

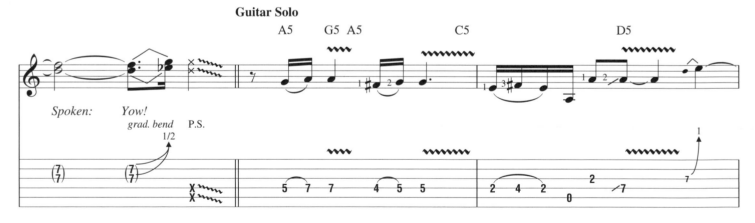

Spoken: *Yow!*

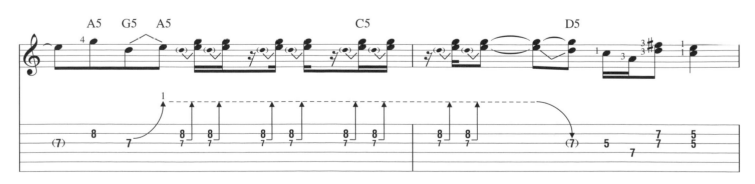

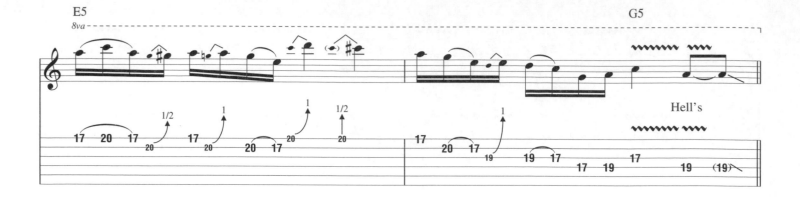

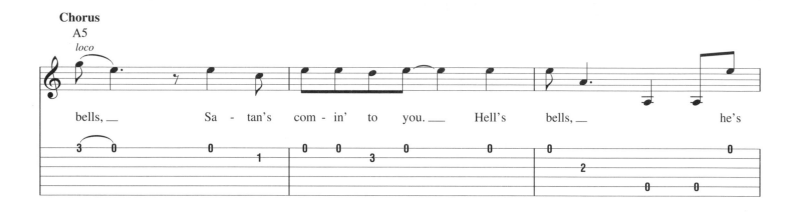

Chorus

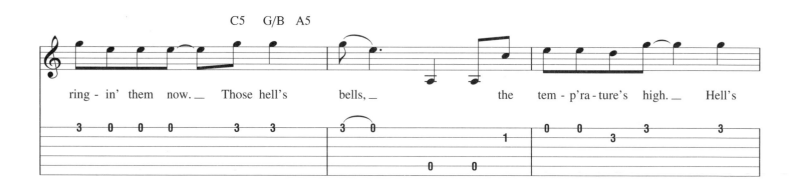

tak - in' you down. ___ Hell's bells, ___ they're drag - gin' you down. ___ Hell's

bells, ___ gon - na split the night. ___ Hell's bells, ___ there's no way to fight, ___ yeah.

Outro

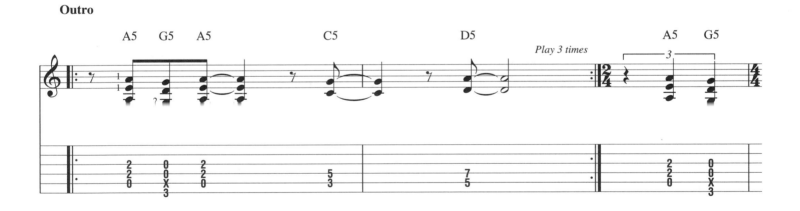

Free time

A tempo

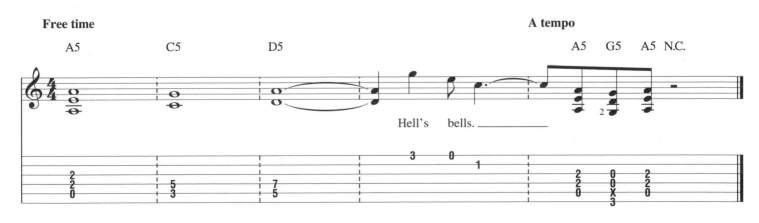

Hell's bells. ___

Highway to Hell

Words and Music by Angus Young, Malcolm Young and Bon Scott

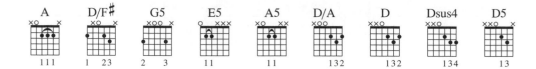

Strum Pattern: 5
Pick Pattern: 1

Intro
Moderate Rock

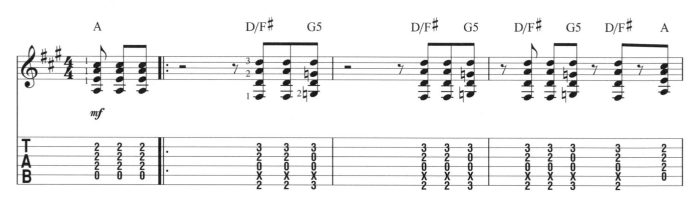

Verse
w/ Intro pattern

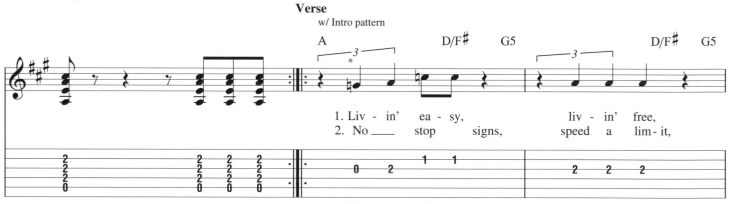

1. Liv - in' ea - sy, liv - in' free,
2. No ___ stop signs, speed a lim - it,

*Sung one octave higher throughout, except where noted.

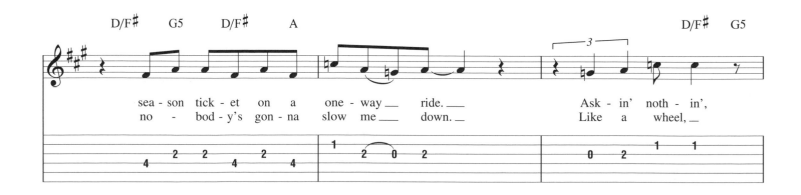

sea - son tick - et on a one - way ___ ride. ___ Ask - in' noth - in',
no - bod - y's gon - na slow me ___ down. ___ Like a wheel, ___

Copyright © 1979 by J. Albert & Son Pty., Ltd.
International Copyright Secured   All Rights Reserved

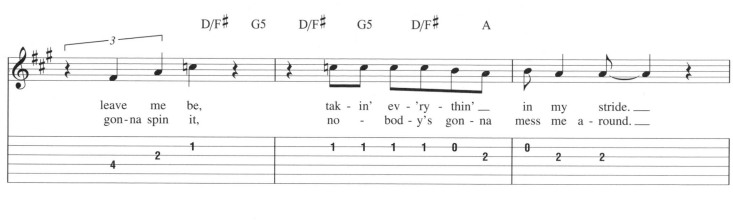

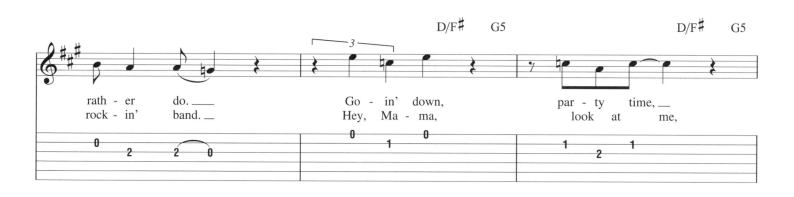

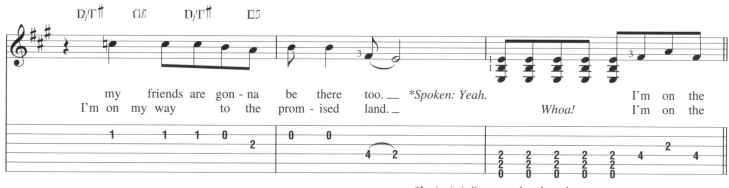

*Lyrics in italics are spoken throughout.

Chorus

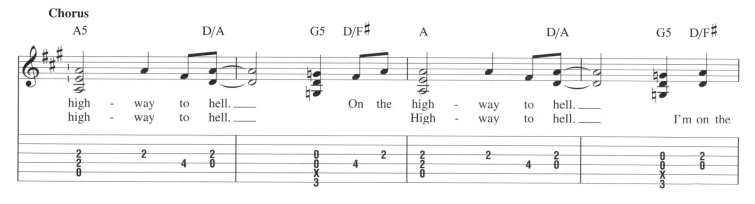

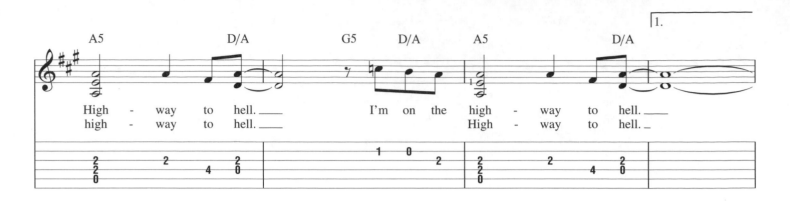

High-way to hell. ___ I'm on the high-way to hell. ___
high-way to hell. ___ High-way to hell. ___

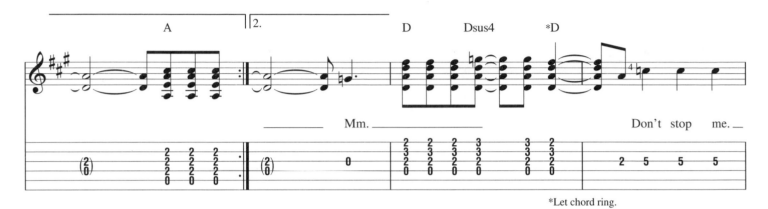

___ Mm. ___ Don't stop me. ___

*Let chord ring.

Guitar Solo

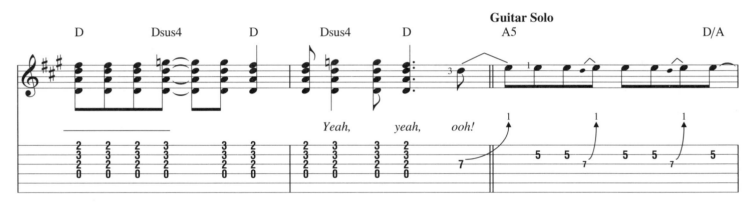

Yeah, yeah, ooh!

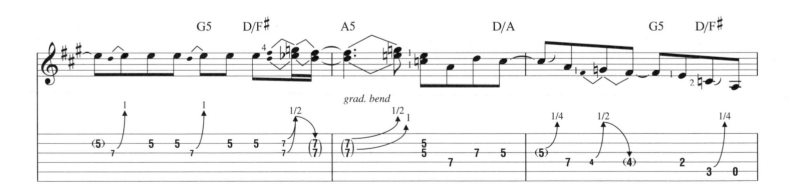

grad. bend

let ring - - - -
hold bend

let ring -

**Barre 4th finger.

Chorus
w/ lead Voc. ad lib. on repeat

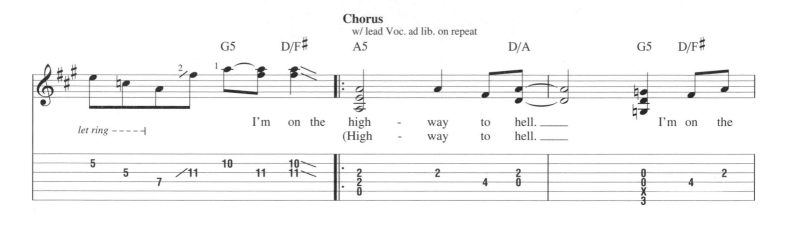

I'm on the high - way to hell. _____ I'm on the

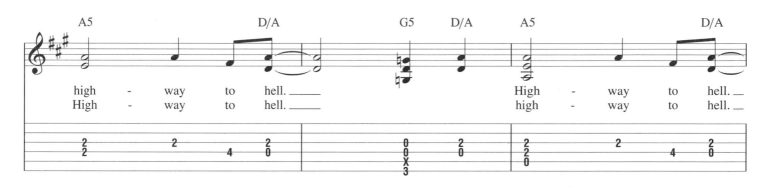

high - way to hell. _____ High - way to hell. _

High - way to hell. _____ high - way to hell. _

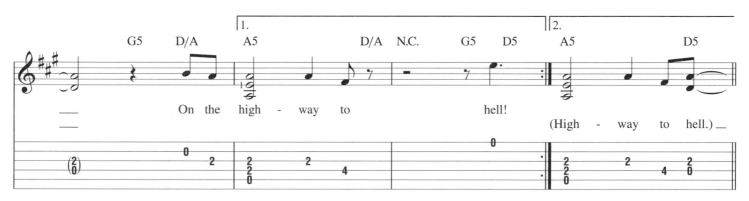

On the high - way to hell!

(High - way to hell.) _

Outro
Free time

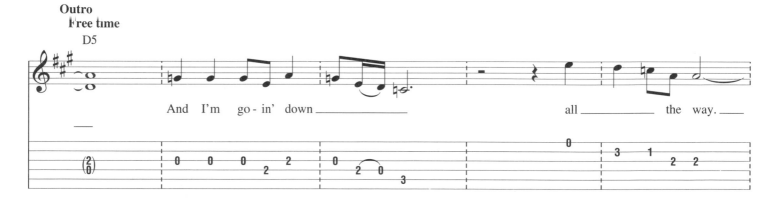

And I'm go- in' down _____ all _____ the way. _____

_____

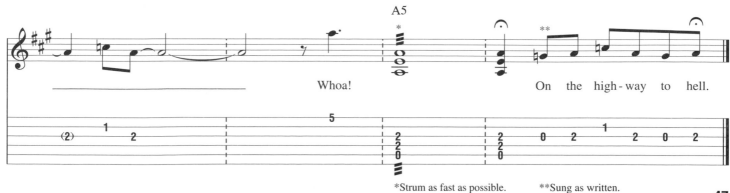

Whoa! On the high-way to hell.

*Strum as fast as possible. **Sung as written.

Let's Get It Up

Words and Music by Angus Young, Malcolm Young and Brian Johnson

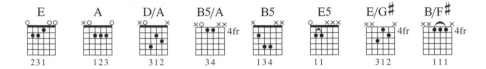

Strum Pattern: 3, 6
Pick Pattern: 3, 4

Intro
Moderate Rock

band enters

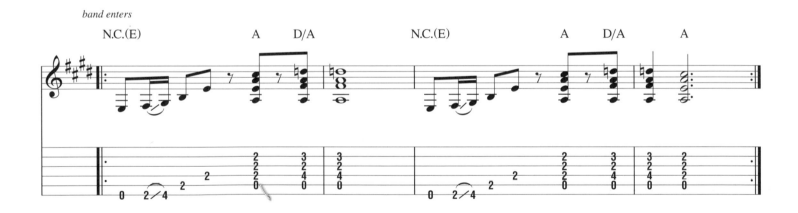

Verse

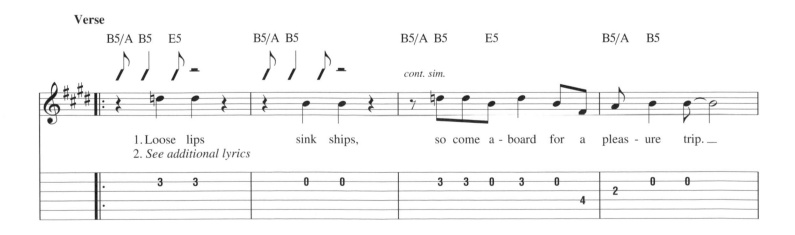

1. Loose lips   sink ships,   so come a-board for a pleas-ure trip. _
2. *See additional lyrics*

Copyright © 1981 by J. Albert & Son Pty., Ltd.
International Copyright Secured   All Rights Reserved

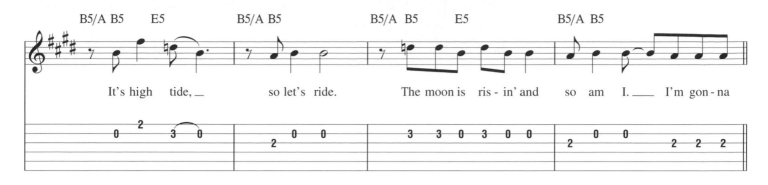

B5/A B5   E5   B5/A B5   B5/A B5   E5   B5/A B5

It's high   tide, __   so let's ride.   The moon is ris - in' and so am I. __ I'm gon - na

Pre-Chorus

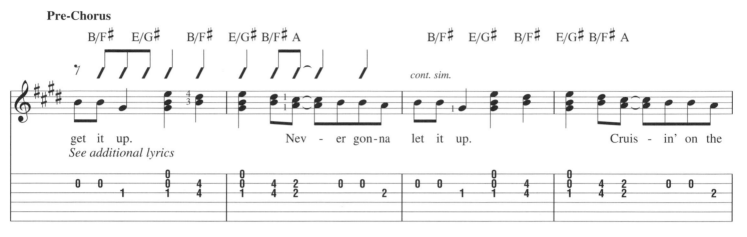

B/F# E/G#   B/F# E/G# B/F# A   B/F#   E/G#   B/F#   E/G# B/F# A

cont. sim.

get it up.   Nev - er gon-na let it up.   Cruis - in' on the
See additional lyrics

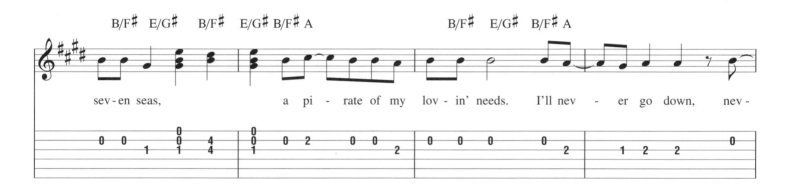

B/F# E/G#   B/F# E/G# B/F# A   B/F#   E/G#   B/F# A

sev - en seas,   a pi - rate of my lov - in' needs. I'll nev - er go down, nev -

Chorus

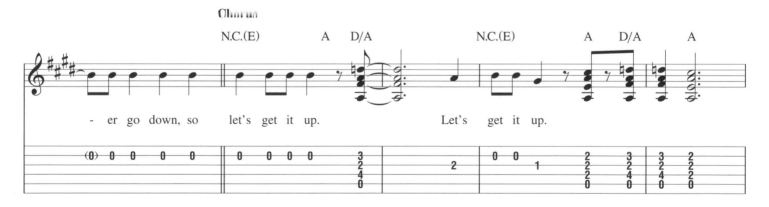

N.C.(E)   A D/A   N.C.(E)   A   D/A   A

- er go down, so let's get it up.   Let's get it up.

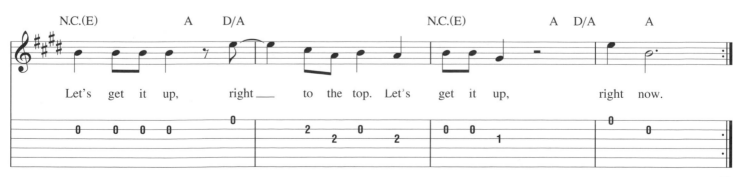

N.C.(E)   A D/A   N.C.(E)   A D/A   A

Let's get it up,   right ___ to the top. Let's get it up,   right now.

Outro

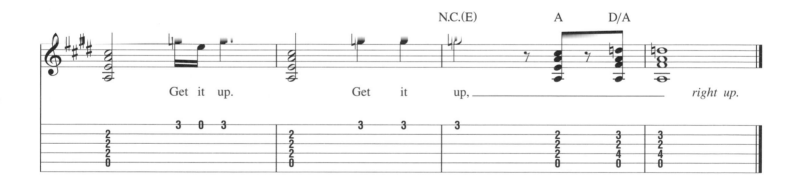

Additional Lyrics

2. Loose wires cause fires,
   Gettin' tangled in my desires.
   So screw 'em up, plug 'em in,
   Then switch it on and start all over again.

Pre-Chorus I'm gonna get it up.
   Never gonna let it up.
   Tickin' like a time bomb,
   Blowin' out the fuse box.
   I'll never go down,
   Never go down, so...

Rock and Roll Ain't Noise Pollution

Words and Music by Angus Young, Malcolm Young and Brian Johnson

Strum Pattern: 3
Pick Pattern: 3

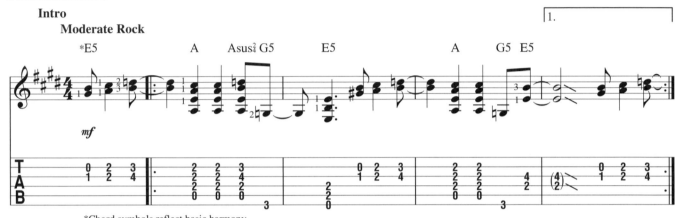

*Chord symbols reflect basic harmony.

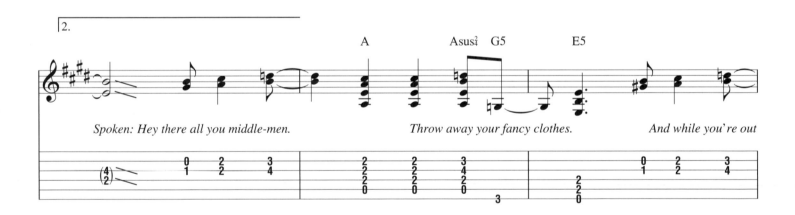

Spoken: Hey there all you middle-men.   *Throw away your fancy clothes.*   *And while you're out*

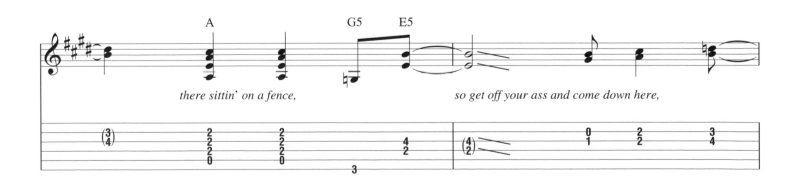

there sittin' on a fence,   *so get off your ass and come down here,*

Copyright © 1980 by J. Albert & Son Pty., Ltd.
International Copyright Secured   All Rights Reserved

'cause rock 'n' roll   ain't no riddle, man.   To me, it makes   good,   good

sense.   Good sense.

Verse

1. Heav - y dec - i - bels are play - in'   on my gui - tar. __ We got vi - bra - tions com - in' up from the   floor. __
2. *See additional lyrics*

*Sung one octave higher throughout.

__ Well, just list - 'nin' to the rock that's giv - in' too much   noise. __ Are you

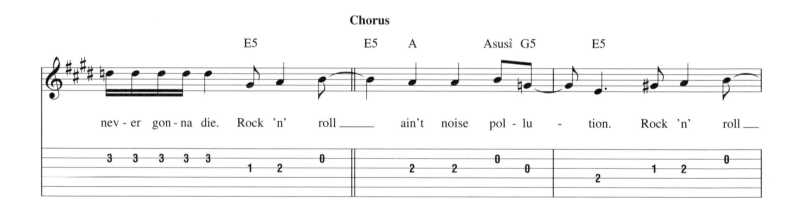

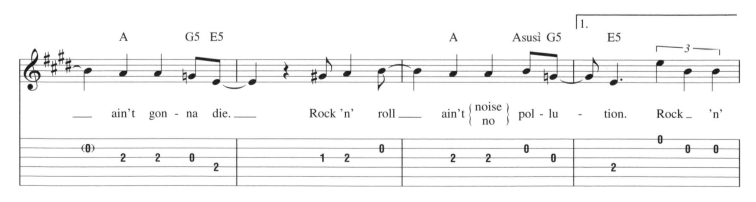

roll, it will sur-vive. ____   -tion. Rock 'n' roll ____ is just   rock 'n' roll. ____

Guitar Solo

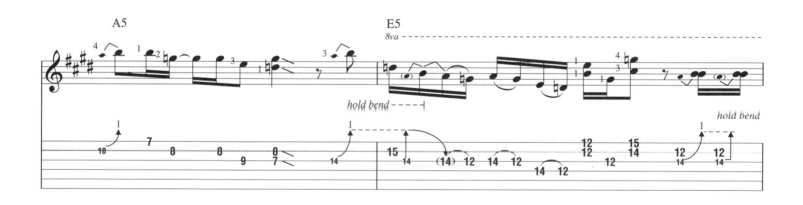

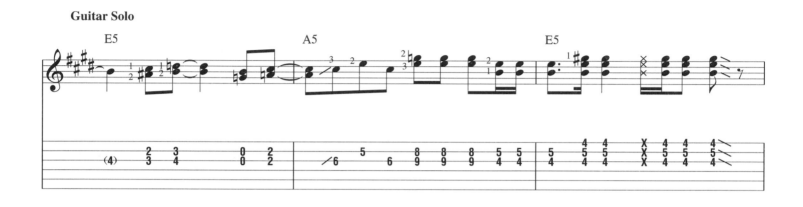

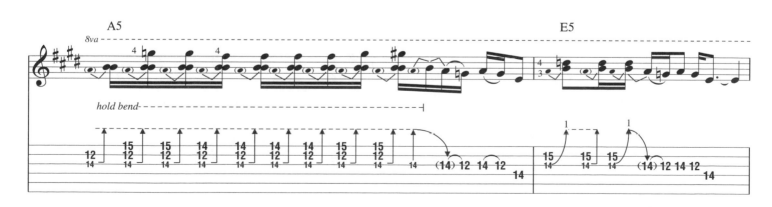

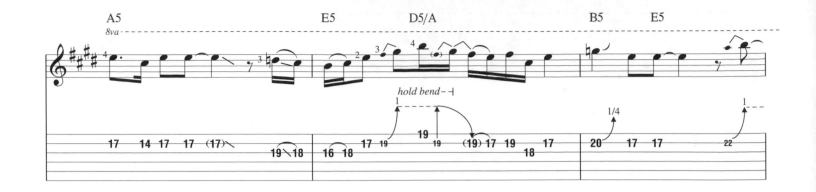

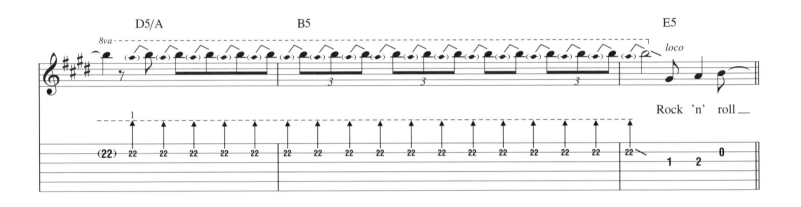

Outro-Chorus

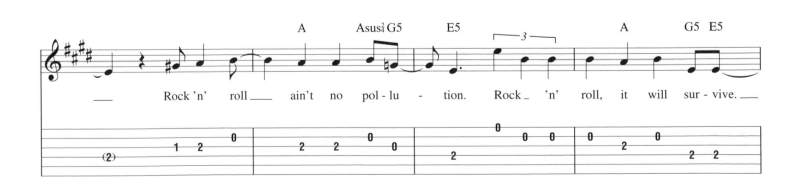

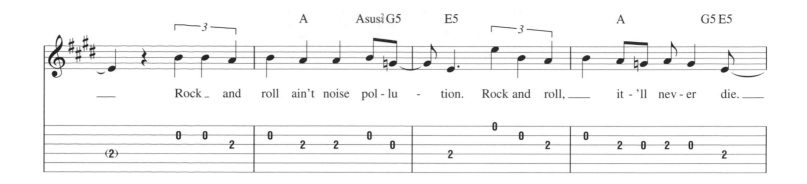

Rock _ and roll ain't noise pol - lu - tion. Rock and roll, ___ it - 'll nev - er die. ___

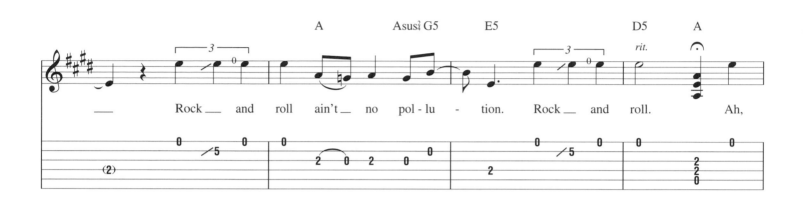

Rock ___ and roll ain't ___ no pol - lu - tion. Rock ___ and roll. Ah,

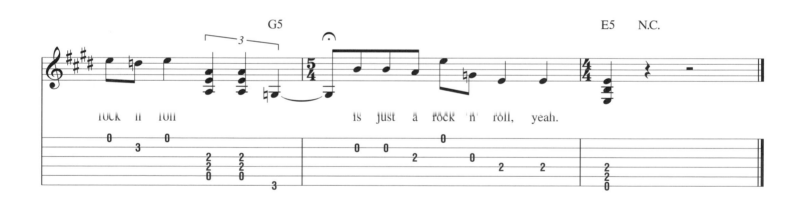

rock 'n' roll is just a rock 'n' roll, yeah.

Additional Lyrics

2. I took a look inside your bedroom door.
   You looked so good lying on your bed.
   Well, I asked you if you wanted any rhythm and love.
   You said you wanna rock 'n' roll instead.

Thunderstruck

Words and Music by Angus Young and Malcolm Young

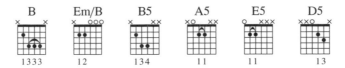

Strum Pattern: 1, 3

Intro

Moderate Rock

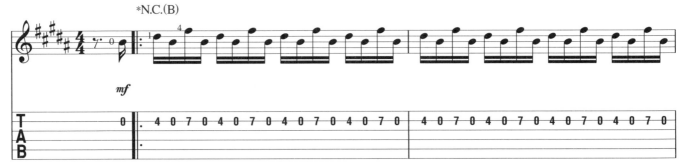

*Chords in parentheses reflect implied harmony.

Copyright © 1990 by J. Albert & Son Pty., Ltd.
International Copyright Secured   All Rights Reserved

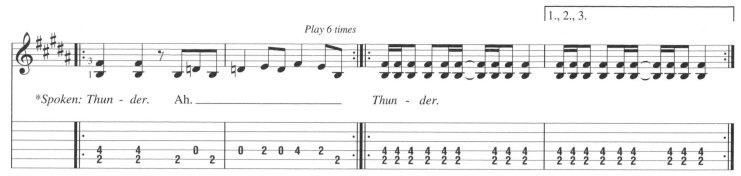

Play 6 times

1., 2., 3.

Spoken: Thun - der. Ah. _____ *Thun - der.*

*Lyrics in italics are spoken throughout.

4.

Verse

B5

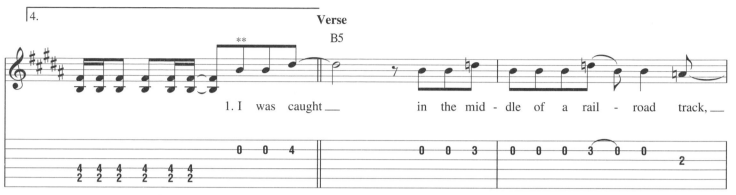

1. I was caught ___ in the mid - dle of a rail - road track, ___

**Sung one octave higher throughout.

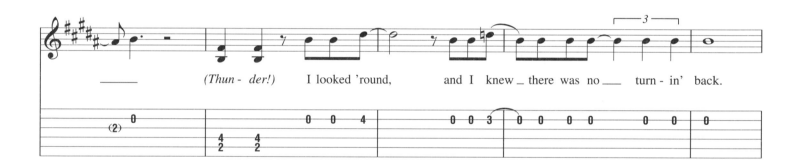

_____ *(Thun - der!)* I looked 'round, and I knew _ there was no ___ turn - in' back.

(Thun - der!) My mind raced, and I thought ___ what _ could I do. _____

(Thun - der!) And I knew ___ there was no _____ help, no help from you.

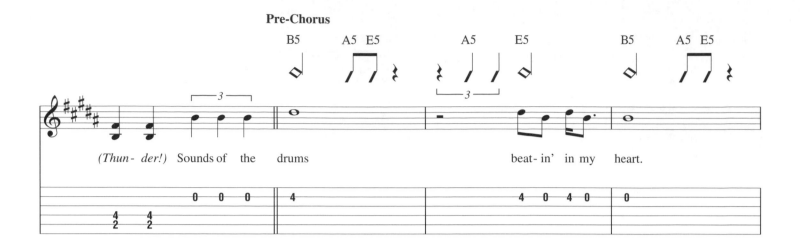

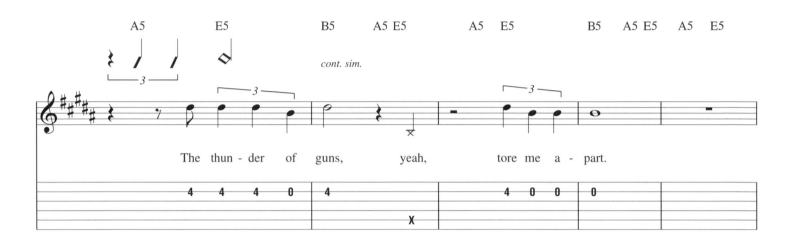

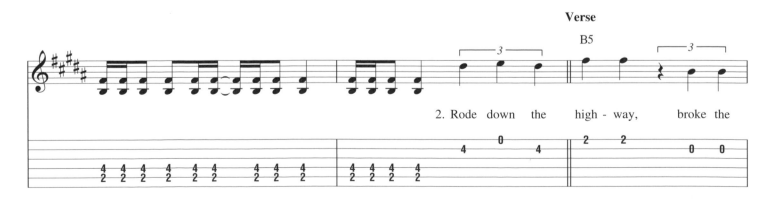

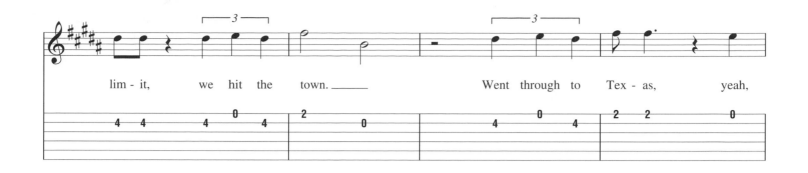

lim - it,   we hit the town. _____   Went through to Tex - as,   yeah,

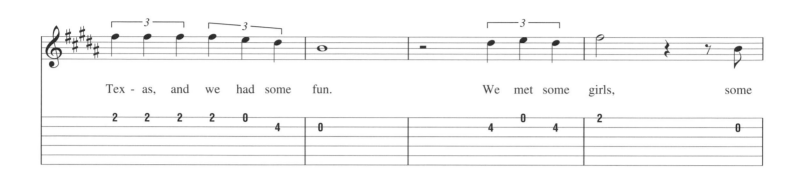

Tex - as,   and we had some fun.   We met some girls,   some

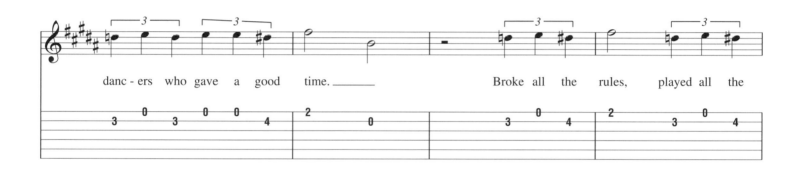

danc - ers who gave a good time. _____   Broke all the rules,   played all the

Pre-Chorus

D5   A5   E5   N.C.

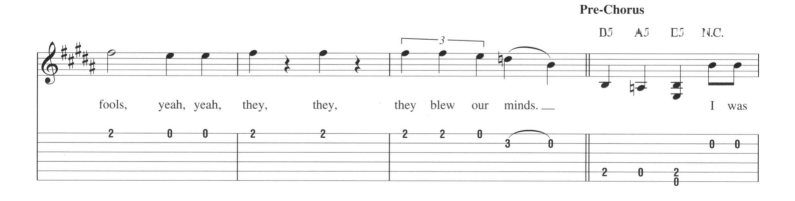

fools,   yeah, yeah, they,   they,   they blew our minds. __   I was

A5   B5   A5   E5   N.C.   A5   B5   A5   E5   N.C.

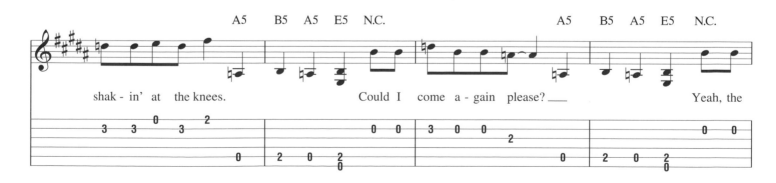

shak - in' at the knees.   Could I come a - gain please? ___   Yeah, the

2.
Outro-Chorus
B5 A5 D5 E5 A5 E5 B5 A5 D5 E5
fine, fine. Thun - der - struck. Yeah, yeah, yeah, thun - der - struck.
A5 E5 B5 A5 D5 E5 A5 E5 B5 A5 D5 E5
Thun - der - struck, thun - der - struck. Whoa, ba - by, ba - by, thun - der - struck.
A5 E5 B5 A5 D5 E5 A5 E5 B5 A5 D5 E5
You've been thun - der - struck. Thun - der - struck.
A5 E5 B5 A5 D5 E5 A5 E5 B5 A5 D5 E5
Thun-der - struck. Thun-der - struck.
A5 E5 B5
rit.
N.C.
You've been thun - der - struck.

T.N.T.

Words and Music by Angus Young, Malcolm Young and Bon Scott

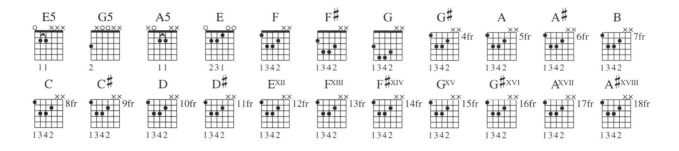

Strum Pattern: 2, 3

Intro
Moderate Rock

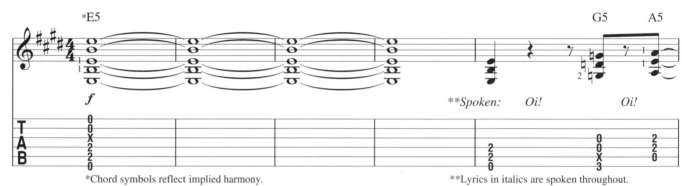

*Chord symbols reflect implied harmony.

**Lyrics in italics are spoken throughout.

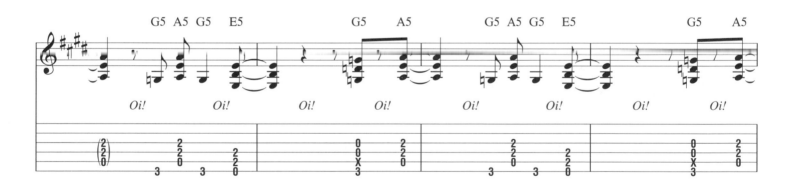

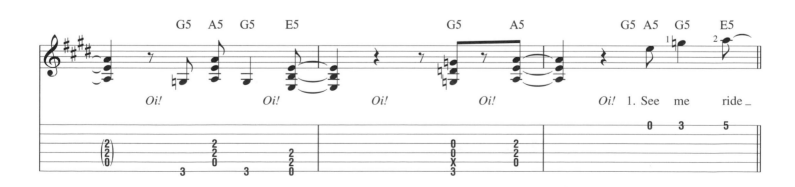

Copyright © 1975 by J. Albert & Son Pty., Ltd.
International Copyright Secured   All Rights Reserved

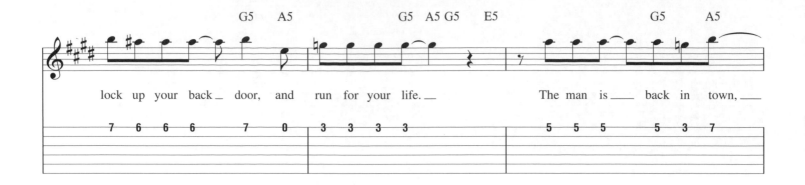

lock up your back door, and run for your life. The man is back in town,

D.S. al Coda 1

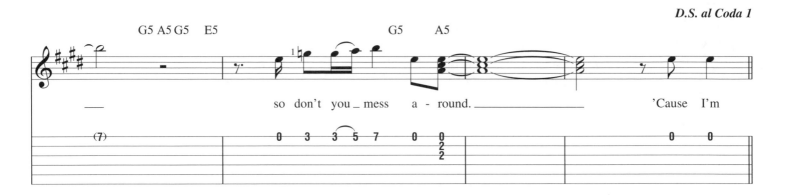

so don't you mess a - round. 'Cause I'm

Coda 1

Guitar Solo

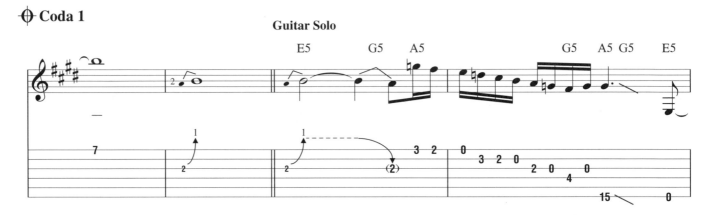

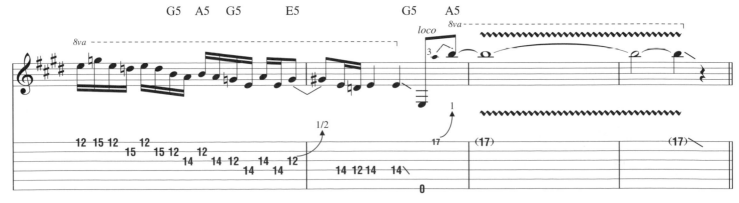

Interlude

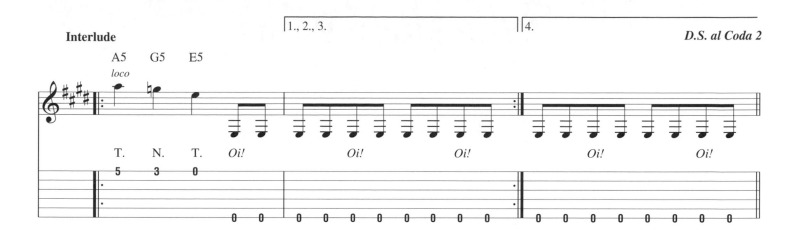

Coda 2

Outro

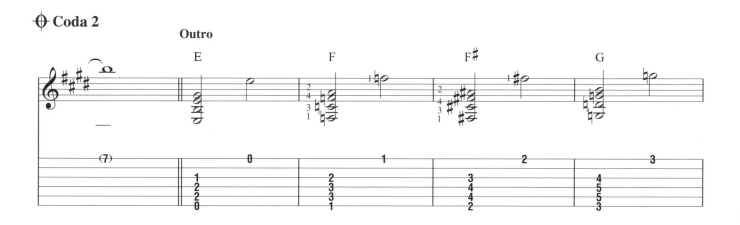

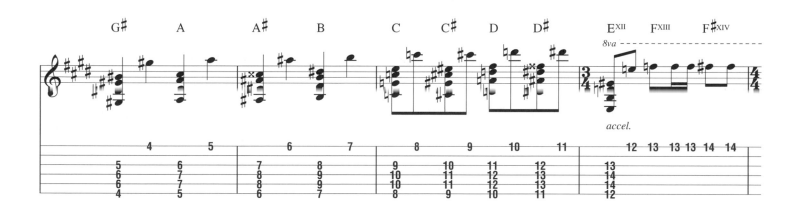

Free Time

Who Made Who

Words and Music by Angus Young, Malcolm Young and Brian Johnson

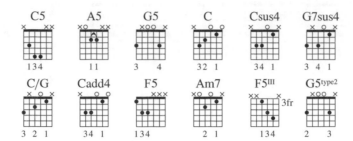

Strum Pattern: 1, 3
Pick Pattern: 2, 4

Intro
Moderate Rock

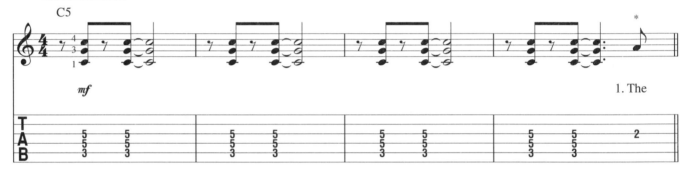

1. The

*Sung one octave
higher throughout.

Verse

vid - e - o games she play __ me.
da - ta bank know my num - ber.

Face it, on the lev - el, but it take you ev - 'ry - time on a
Says I got - ta pay 'cause I made the grade __ last year. __

one - on - one. __
__

Feel it run - nin' down your spine. __
Feel it when I turn the screw. __

Copyright © 1986 by J. Albert & Son Pty., Ltd.
International Copyright Secured All Rights Reserved

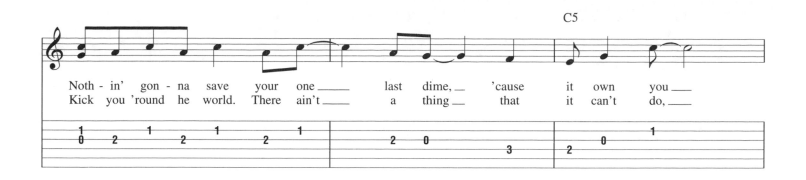

Noth - in' gon - na save your one ____ last dime, ____ 'cause it own you ____
Kick you 'round he world. There ain't ____ a thing ____ that it can't do, ____

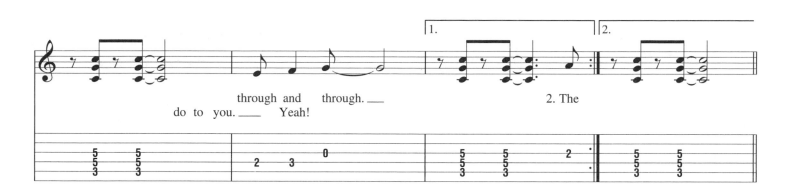

through and through. ____
do to you. ____ Yeah!

2. The

𝄋 Chorus

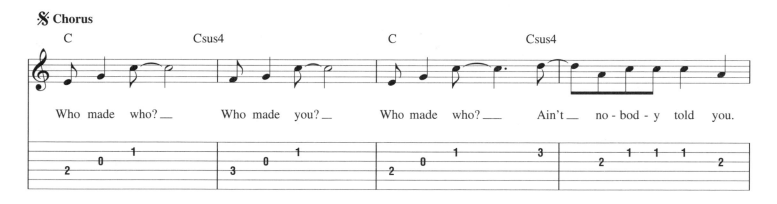

Who made who? __ Who made you? __ Who made who? ____ Ain't __ no - bod - y told you.

Who made who? __ Who made you? __ If you made them and they __ made you,

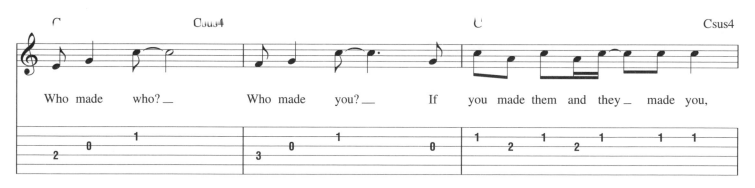

To Coda ⊕

who pick up __ the mid - dle and who __ made __ who?

Spoken: Yeah!

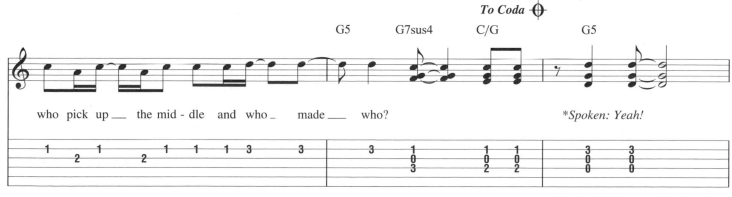

*Lyrics in italics are spoken throughout.

71

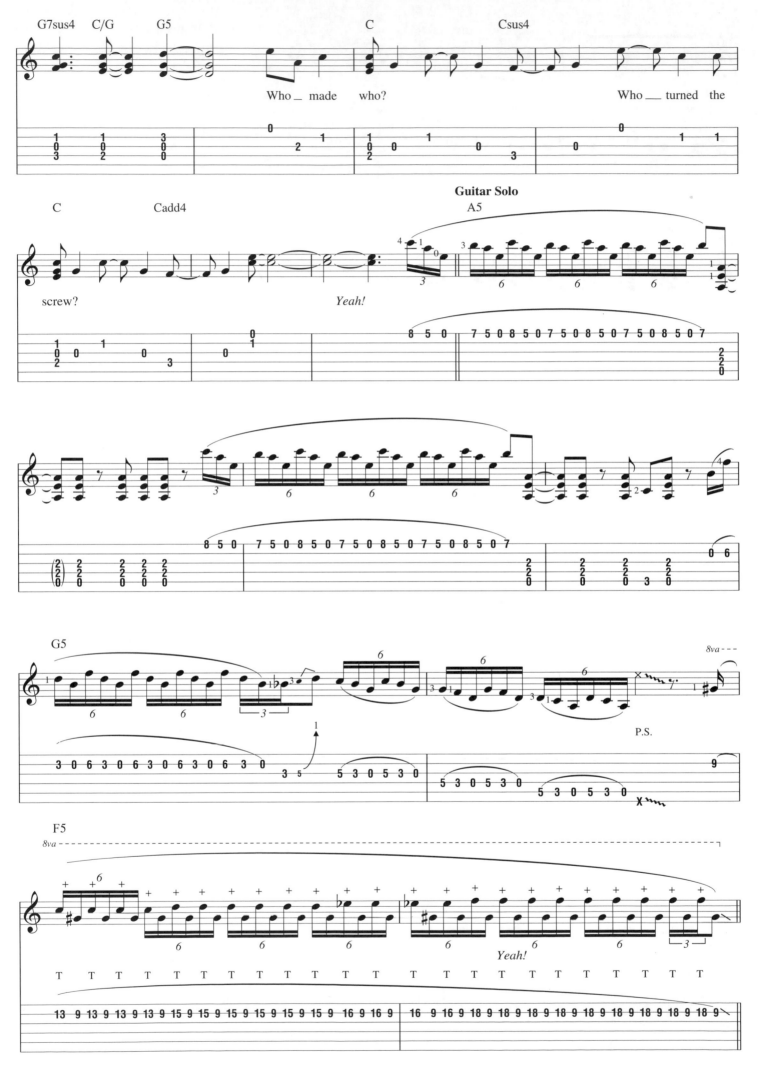

Verse

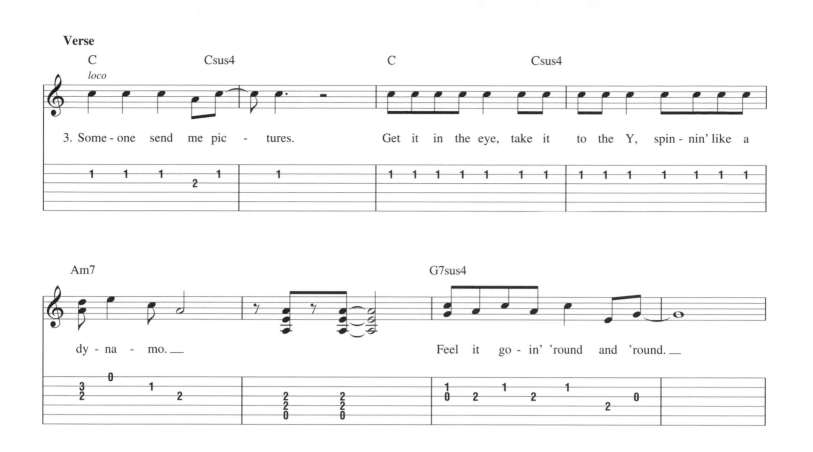

3. Some-one send me pic - tures. Get it in the eye, take it to the Y, spin-nin' like a

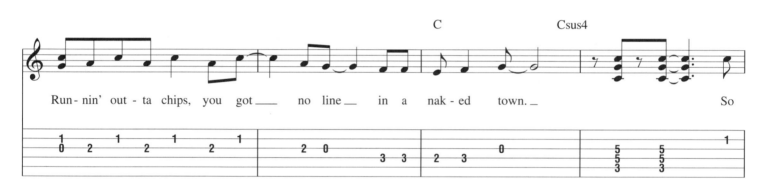

dy - na - mo. ___ Feel it go-in' 'round and 'round. ___

Run-nin' out-ta chips, you got ___ no line ___ in a nak-ed town. ___ So

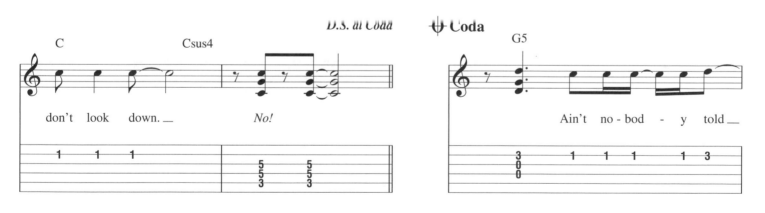

don't look down. ___ *No!*   *D.S. al Coda*   **Coda**   Ain't no-bod - y told ___

___ you.   *Oh!*   Who made who? ___

Whole Lotta Rosie

Words and Music by Angus Young, Malcolm Young and Bon Scott

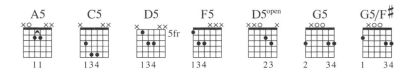

Strum Pattern: 1, 6
Pick Pattern: 4, 6

Intro
Moderately fast Rock

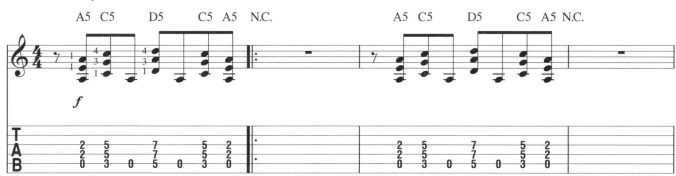

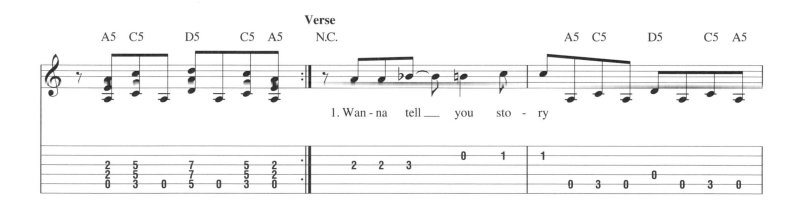

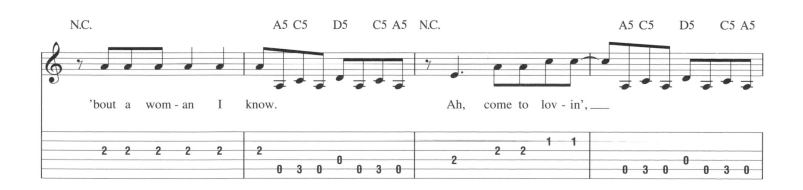

Copyright © 1977 by J. Albert & Son Pty., Ltd.
International Copyright Secured   All Rights Reserved

she steals the show. ___ She ain't ex-act-ly pret-ty, _____

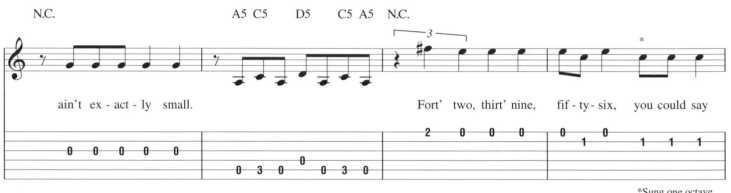

ain't ex-act-ly small. Fort' two, thirt' nine, fif-ty-six, you could say

*Sung one octave
higher till end.

Interlude

1., 2., 3.

she's got it all. _____

Verse

4.

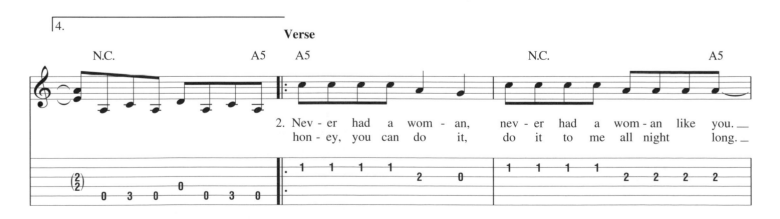

2. Nev - er had a wom - an, nev - er had a wom-an like you. ___
hon - ey, you can do it, do it to me all night long. ___

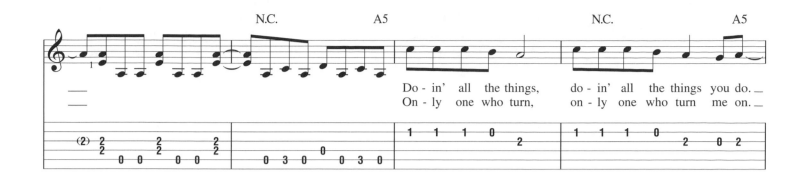

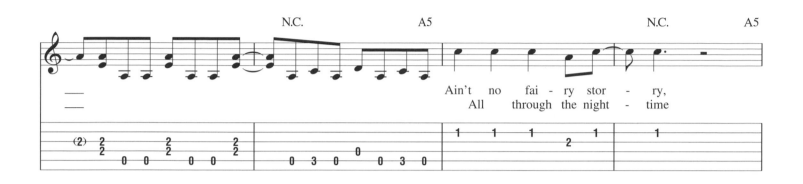

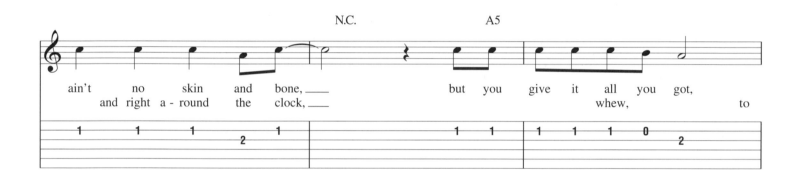

%́ Chorus

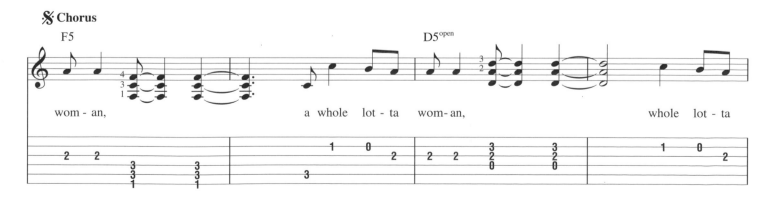

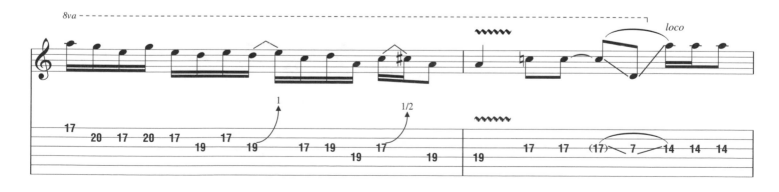

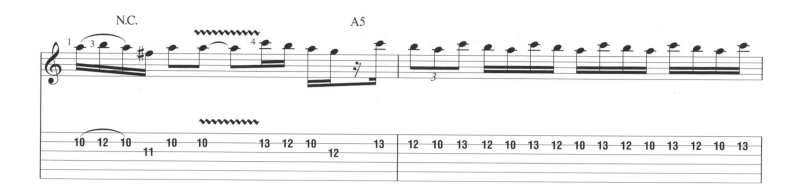

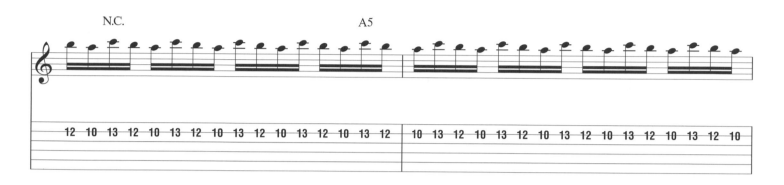

D.S. al Coda

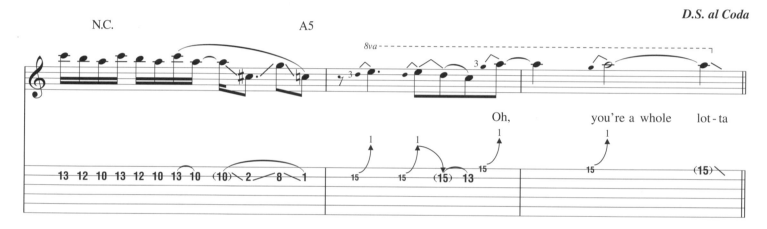

Oh,   you're a whole   lot - ta

Coda

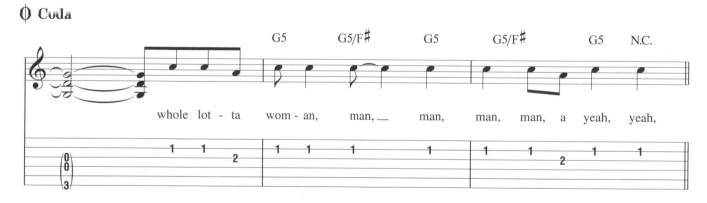

whole lot - ta   wom - an,   man,   man,   man, man, a yeah,   yeah,

Outro-Guitar Solo
w/ Voc. ad lib.

Repeat and fade

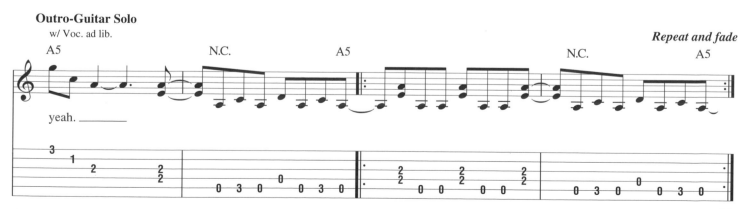

yeah. _____

You Shook Me All Night Long

Words and Music by Angus Young, Malcolm Young and Brian Johnson

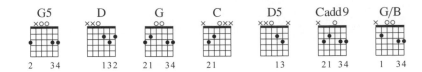

Strum Pattern: 1

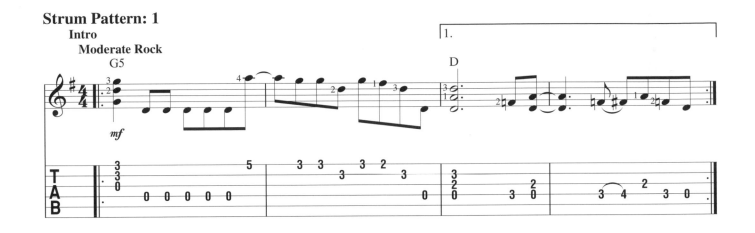

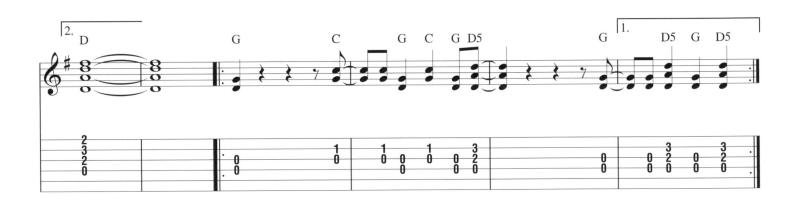

1. She was a fast ma-chine, she kept her mo-tor clean, she was the

2. *See additional lyrics*

Copyright © 1980 J. Albert & Son Pty., Ltd.
International Copyright Secured All Rights Reserved

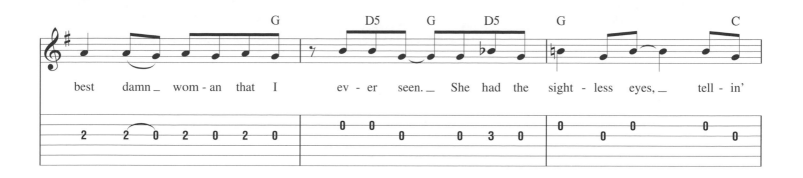

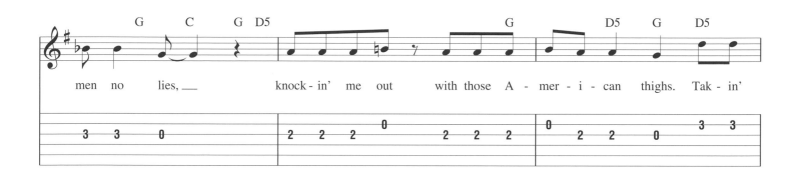

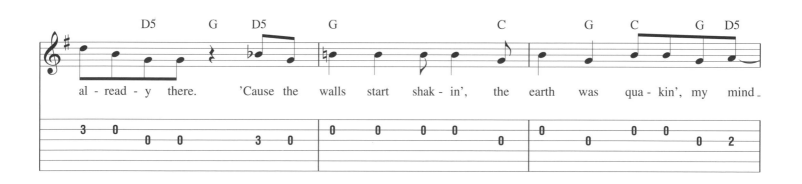

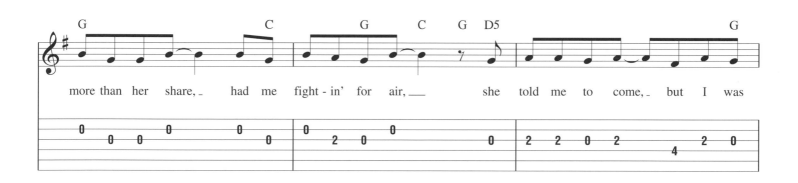

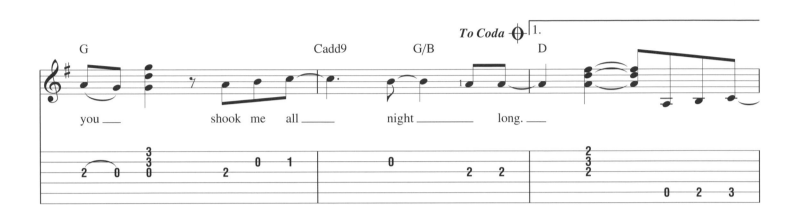

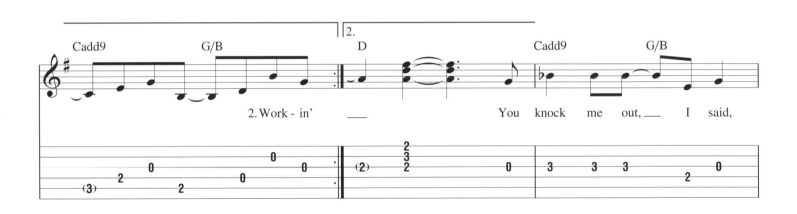

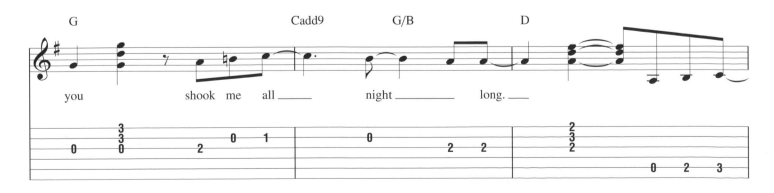

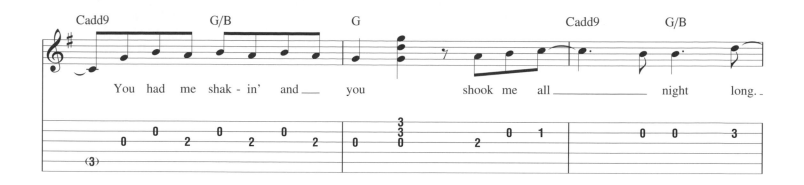

You had me shak-in' and ___ you shook me all _____ night long. _

_____ Yeah, you shook _ me, the way you shook _ me.

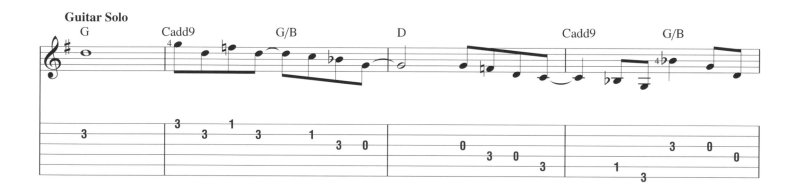

Guitar Solo

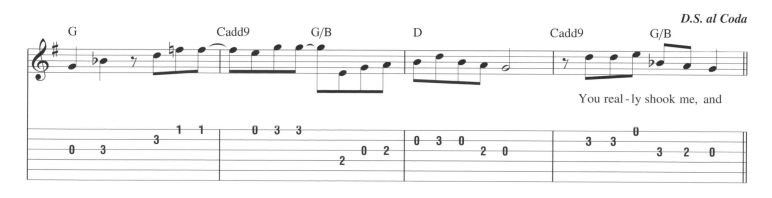

D.S. al Coda

You real-ly shook me, and

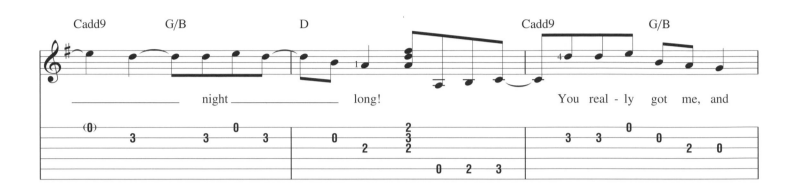

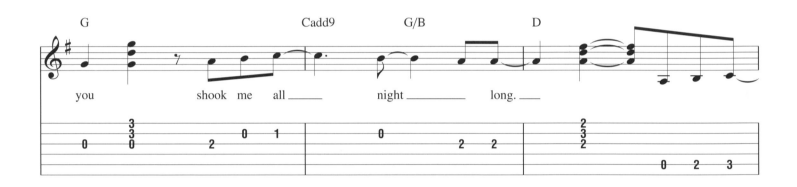

Additional Lyrics

2. Workin' double-time on the seduction line,
She was one of a kind, she's just mine all mine.
She wanted no applause, just another course,
Made a meal out of me and came back for more.
Had to cool me down to take another round,
Now I'm back in the ring to take another swing,
'Cause the walls were shakin', the earth was quakin',
My mind was achin', and we were makin' it.

EASY GUITAR WITH NOTES & TAB

This series features simplified arrangements with notes, tab, chord charts, and strum and pick patterns.

MIXED FOLIOS

00702287	Acoustic	$19.99
00702002	Acoustic Rock Hits for Easy Guitar	$15.99
00702166	All-Time Best Guitar Collection	$19.99
00702232	Best Acoustic Songs for Easy Guitar	$16.99
00119835	Best Children's Songs	$16.99
00703055	The Big Book of Nursery Rhymes & Children's Songs	$16.99
00698978	Big Christmas Collection	$19.99
00702394	Bluegrass Songs for Easy Guitar	$15.99
00289632	Bohemian Rhapsody	$19.99
00703387	Celtic Classics	$14.99
00224808	Chart Hits of 2016-2017	$14.99
00267383	Chart Hits of 2017-2018	$14.99
00334293	Chart Hits of 2019-2020	$16.99
00702149	Children's Christian Songbook	$9.99
00702028	Christmas Classics	$8.99
00101779	Christmas Guitar	$14.99
00702141	Classic Rock	$8.95
00159642	Classical Melodies	$12.99
00253933	Disney/Pixar's Coco	$16.99
00702203	CMT's 100 Greatest Country Songs	$34.99
00702283	The Contemporary Christian Collection	$16.99
00196954	Contemporary Disney	$19.99
00702239	Country Classics for Easy Guitar	$24.99

00702257	Easy Acoustic Guitar Songs	$16.99
00702041	Favorite Hymns for Easy Guitar	$12.99
00222701	Folk Pop Songs	$17.99
00126894	Frozen	$14.99
00333922	Frozen 2	$14.99
00702286	Glee	$16.99
00702160	The Great American Country Songbook	$19.99
00702148	Great American Gospel for Guitar	$14.99
00702050	Great Classical Themes for Easy Guitar	$9.99
00275088	The Greatest Showman	$17.99
00148030	Halloween Guitar Songs	$14.99
00702273	Irish Songs	$12.99
00192503	Jazz Classics for Easy Guitar	$16.99
00702275	Jazz Favorites for Easy Guitar	$17.99
00702274	Jazz Standards for Easy Guitar	$19.99
00702162	Jumbo Easy Guitar Songbook	$24.99
00232285	La La Land	$16.99
00702258	Legends of Rock	$14.99
00702189	MTV's 100 Greatest Pop Songs	$34.99
00702272	1950s Rock	$16.99
00702271	1960s Rock	$16.99
00702270	1970s Rock	$19.99
00702269	1980s Rock	$15.99
00702268	1990s Rock	$19.99
00369043	Rock Songs for Kids	$14.99

00109725	Once	$14.99
00702187	Selections from O Brother Where Art Thou?	$19.99
00702178	100 Songs for Kids	$14.99
00702515	Pirates of the Caribbean	$17.99
00702125	Praise and Worship for Guitar	$14.99
00287930	Songs from *A Star Is Born, The Greatest Showman, La La Land*, and More Movie Musicals	$16.99
00702285	Southern Rock Hits	$12.99
00156420	Star Wars Music	$16.99
00121535	30 Easy Celtic Guitar Solos	$16.99
00702156	3-Chord Rock	$12.99
00244654	Top Hits of 2017	$14.99
00283786	Top Hits of 2018	$14.99
00702294	Top Worship Hits	$17.99
00702255	VH1's 100 Greatest Hard Rock Songs	$34.99
00702175	VH1's 100 Greatest Songs of Rock and Roll	$29.99
00702253	Wicked	$12.99

ARTIST COLLECTIONS

00702267	AC/DC for Easy Guitar	$16.99
00702598	Adele for Easy Guitar	$15.99
00156221	Adele – 25	$16.99
00702040	Best of the Allman Brothers	$16.99
00702865	J.S. Bach for Easy Guitar	$15.99
00702169	Best of The Beach Boys	$15.99
00702292	The Beatles — 1	$22.99
00125796	Best of Chuck Berry	$15.99
00702201	The Essential Black Sabbath	$15.99
00702250	blink-182 — Greatest Hits	$17.99
02501615	Zac Brown Band — The Foundation	$17.99
02501621	Zac Brown Band — You Get What You Give	$16.99
00702043	Best of Johnny Cash	$17.99
00702090	Eric Clapton's Best	$16.99
00702086	Eric Clapton — from the Album Unplugged	$17.99
00702202	The Essential Eric Clapton	$17.99
00702053	Best of Patsy Cline	$15.99
00222697	Very Best of Coldplay – 2nd Edition	$16.99
00702229	The Very Best of Creedence Clearwater Revival	$16.99
00702145	Best of Jim Croce	$16.99
00702278	Crosby, Stills & Nash	$12.99
14042809	Bob Dylan	$15.99
00702276	Fleetwood Mac — Easy Guitar Collection	$17.99
00139462	The Very Best of Grateful Dead	$16.99
00702136	Best of Merle Haggard	$16.99
00702227	Jimi Hendrix — Smash Hits	$19.99
00702288	Best of Hillsong United	$12.99
00702236	Best of Antonio Carlos Jobim	$15.99
00702245	Elton John — Greatest Hits 1970–2002	$19.99

00129855	Jack Johnson	$16.99
00702204	Robert Johnson	$14.99
00702234	Selections from Toby Keith — 35 Biggest Hits	$12.95
00702003	Kiss	$16.99
00702216	Lynyrd Skynyrd	$16.99
00702182	The Essential Bob Marley	$16.99
00146081	Maroon 5	$14.99
00121925	Bruno Mars – Unorthodox Jukebox	$12.99
00702248	Paul McCartney — All the Best	$14.99
00125484	The Best of MercyMe	$12.99
00702209	Steve Miller Band — Young Hearts (Greatest Hits)	$12.95
00124167	Jason Mraz	$15.99
00702096	Best of Nirvana	$16.99
00702211	The Offspring — Greatest Hits	$17.99
00138026	One Direction	$17.99
00702030	Best of Roy Orbison	$17.99
00702144	Best of Ozzy Osbourne	$14.99
00702279	Tom Petty	$17.99
00102911	Pink Floyd	$17.99
00702139	Elvis Country Favorites	$19.99
00702293	The Very Best of Prince	$19.99
00699415	Best of Queen for Guitar	$16.99
00109279	Best of R.E.M.	$14.99
00702208	Red Hot Chili Peppers — Greatest Hits	$16.99
00198960	The Rolling Stones	$17.99
00174793	The Very Best of Santana	$16.99
00702196	Best of Bob Seger	$16.99
00146046	Ed Sheeran	$15.99
00702252	Frank Sinatra — Nothing But the Best	$12.99
00702010	Best of Rod Stewart	$17.99
00702049	Best of George Strait	$17.99

00702259	Taylor Swift for Easy Guitar	$15.99
00359800	Taylor Swift – Easy Guitar Anthology	$24.99
00702260	Taylor Swift — Fearless	$14.99
00139927	Taylor Swift — 1989	$17.99
00115960	Taylor Swift — Red	$16.99
00253667	Taylor Swift — Reputation	$17.99
00702290	Taylor Swift — Speak Now	$16.99
00232849	Chris Tomlin Collection – 2nd Edition	$14.99
00702226	Chris Tomlin — See the Morning	$12.95
00148643	Train	$14.99
00702427	U2 — 18 Singles	$19.99
00702108	Best of Stevie Ray Vaughan	$17.99
00279005	The Who	$14.99
00702123	Best of Hank Williams	$15.99
00194548	Best of John Williams	$14.99
00702228	Neil Young — Greatest Hits	$17.99
00119133	Neil Young — Harvest	$14.99

Prices, contents and availability subject to change without notice.

HAL•LEONARD®

Visit Hal Leonard online at **halleonard.com**

1221
306

HAL•LEONARD® GUITAR PLAY-ALONG

Complete song lists available online.

This series will help you play your favorite songs quickly and easily. Just follow the tab and listen to the audio to the hear how the guitar should sound, and then play along using the separate backing tracks. Audio files also include software to slow down the tempo without changing pitch. The melody and lyrics are included in the book so that you can sing or simply follow along.

INCLUDES TAB

VOL. 1 – ROCK	00699570 / $17.99
VOL. 2 – ACOUSTIC	00699569 / $16.99
VOL. 3 – HARD ROCK	00699573 / $17.99
VOL. 4 – POP/ROCK	00699571 / $16.99
VOL. 5 – THREE CHORD SONGS	00300985 / $16.99
VOL. 6 – '90S ROCK	00298615 / $16.99
VOL. 7 – BLUES	00699575 / $19.99
VOL. 8 – ROCK	00699585 / $16.99
VOL. 9 – EASY ACOUSTIC SONGS	00151708 / $16.99
VOL. 10 – ACOUSTIC	00699586 / $16.95
VOL. 11 – EARLY ROCK	00699579 / $15.99
VOL. 12 – ROCK POP	00291724 / $16.99
VOL. 14 – BLUES ROCK	00699582 / $16.99
VOL. 15 – R&B	00699583 / $17.99
VOL. 16 – JAZZ	00699584 / $16.99
VOL. 17 – COUNTRY	00699588 / $17.99
VOL. 18 – ACOUSTIC ROCK	00699577 / $15.95
VOL. 20 – ROCKABILLY	00699580 / $17.99
VOL. 21 – SANTANA	00174525 / $17.99
VOL. 22 – CHRISTMAS	00699600 / $15.99
VOL. 23 – SURF	00699635 / $17.99
VOL. 24 – ERIC CLAPTON	00699649 / $19.99
VOL. 25 – THE BEATLES	00198265 / $19.99
VOL. 26 – ELVIS PRESLEY	00699643 / $16.99
VOL. 27 – DAVID LEE ROTH	00699645 / $16.95
VOL. 28 – GREG KOCH	00699646 / $19.99
VOL. 29 – BOB SEGER	00699647 / $16.99
VOL. 30 – KISS	00699644 / $17.99
VOL. 32 – THE OFFSPRING	00699653 / $14.95
VOL. 33 – ACOUSTIC CLASSICS	00699656 / $19.99
VOL. 34 – CLASSIC ROCK	00699658 / $17.99
VOL. 35 – HAIR METAL	00699660 / $17.99
VOL. 36 – SOUTHERN ROCK	00699661 / $19.99
VOL. 37 – ACOUSTIC UNPLUGGED	00699662 / $22.99
VOL. 38 – BLUES	00699663 / $17.99
VOL. 39 – '80s METAL	00699664 / $17.99
VOL. 40 – INCUBUS	00699668 / $17.95
VOL. 41 – ERIC CLAPTON	00699669 / $17.99
VOL. 42 – COVER BAND HITS	00211597 / $16.99
VOL. 43 – LYNYRD SKYNYRD	00699681 / $22.99
VOL. 44 – JAZZ GREATS	00699689 / $16.99
VOL. 45 – TV THEMES	00699718 / $14.95
VOL. 46 – MAINSTREAM ROCK	00699722 / $16.95
VOL. 47 – JIMI HENDRIX SMASH HITS	00699723 / $19.99
VOL. 48 – AEROSMITH CLASSICS	00699724 / $17.99
VOL. 49 – STEVIE RAY VAUGHAN	00699725 / $17.99
VOL. 50 – VAN HALEN: 1978-1984	00110269 / $19.99
VOL. 51 – ALTERNATIVE '90s	00699727 / $14.99
VOL. 52 – FUNK	00699728 / $15.99
VOL. 53 – DISCO	00699729 / $14.99
VOL. 54 – HEAVY METAL	00699730 / $17.99
VOL. 55 – POP METAL	00699731 / $14.95
VOL. 57 – GUNS 'N' ROSES	00159922 / $19.99
VOL. 58 – BLINK 182	00699772 / $17.99
VOL. 59 – CHET ATKINS	00702347 / $17.99
VOL. 60 – 3 DOORS DOWN	00699774 / $14.95
VOL. 62 – CHRISTMAS CAROLS	00699798 / $12.95
VOL. 63 – CREEDENCE CLEARWATER REVIVAL	00699802 / $17.99
VOL. 64 – ULTIMATE OZZY OSBOURNE	00699803 / $19.99
VOL. 66 – THE ROLLING STONES	00699807 / $19.99
VOL. 67 – BLACK SABBATH	00699808 / $17.99
VOL. 68 – PINK FLOYD – DARK SIDE OF THE MOON	00699809 / $17.99
VOL. 71 – CHRISTIAN ROCK	00699824 / $14.95

VOL. 73 – BLUESY ROCK	00699829 / $17.99
VOL. 74 – SIMPLE STRUMMING SONGS	00151706 / $19.99
VOL. 75 – TOM PETTY	00699882 / $19.99
VOL. 76 – COUNTRY HITS	00699884 / $16.99
VOL. 77 – BLUEGRASS	00699910 / $17.99
VOL. 78 – NIRVANA	00700132 / $17.99
VOL. 79 – NEIL YOUNG	00700133 / $24.99
VOL. 81 – ROCK ANTHOLOGY	00700176 / $22.99
VOL. 82 – EASY ROCK SONGS	00700177 / $17.99
VOL. 84 – STEELY DAN	00700200 / $19.99
VOL. 85 – THE POLICE	00700269 / $16.99
VOL. 86 – BOSTON	00700465 / $19.99
VOL. 87 – ACOUSTIC WOMEN	00700763 / $14.99
VOL. 88 – GRUNGE	00700467 / $16.99
VOL. 89 – REGGAE	00700468 / $15.99
VOL. 90 – CLASSICAL POP	00700469 / $14.99
VOL. 91 – BLUES INSTRUMENTALS	00700505 / $19.99
VOL. 92 – EARLY ROCK INSTRUMENTALS	00700506 / $17.99
VOL. 93 – ROCK INSTRUMENTALS	00700507 / $17.99
VOL. 94 – SLOW BLUES	00700508 / $16.99
VOL. 95 – BLUES CLASSICS	00700509 / $15.99
VOL. 96 – BEST COUNTRY HITS	00211615 / $16.99
VOL. 97 – CHRISTMAS CLASSICS	00236542 / $14.99
VOL. 99 – ZZ TOP	00700762 / $16.99
VOL. 100 – B.B. KING	00700466 / $16.99
VOL. 101 – SONGS FOR BEGINNERS	00701917 / $14.99
VOL. 102 – CLASSIC PUNK	00700769 / $14.99
VOL. 104 – DUANE ALLMAN	00700846 / $22.99
VOL. 105 – LATIN	00700939 / $16.99
VOL. 106 – WEEZER	00700958 / $17.99
VOL. 107 – CREAM	00701069 / $17.99
VOL. 108 – THE WHO	00701053 / $17.99
VOL. 109 – STEVE MILLER	00701054 / $19.99
VOL. 110 – SLIDE GUITAR HITS	00701055 / $17.99
VOL. 111 – JOHN MELLENCAMP	00701056 / $14.99
VOL. 112 – QUEEN	00701052 / $16.99
VOL. 113 – JIM CROCE	00701058 / $19.99
VOL. 114 – BON JOVI	00701060 / $17.99
VOL. 115 – JOHNNY CASH	00701070 / $17.99
VOL. 116 – THE VENTURES	00701124 / $17.99
VOL. 117 – BRAD PAISLEY	00701224 / $16.99
VOL. 118 – ERIC JOHNSON	00701353 / $17.99
VOL. 119 – AC/DC CLASSICS	00701356 / $19.99
VOL. 120 – PROGRESSIVE ROCK	00701457 / $14.99
VOL. 121 – U2	00701508 / $17.99
VOL. 122 – CROSBY, STILLS & NASH	00701610 / $16.99
VOL. 123 – LENNON & McCARTNEY ACOUSTIC	00701614 / $16.99
VOL. 124 – SMOOTH JAZZ	00200664 / $16.99
VOL. 125 – JEFF BECK	00701687 / $19.99
VOL. 126 – BOB MARLEY	00701701 / $17.99
VOL. 127 – 1970s ROCK	00701739 / $17.99
VOL. 128 – 1960s ROCK	00701740 / $14.99
VOL. 129 – MEGADETH	00701741 / $17.99
VOL. 130 – IRON MAIDEN	00701742 / $17.99
VOL. 131 – 1990s ROCK	00701743 / $14.99
VOL. 132 – COUNTRY ROCK	00701757 / $15.99
VOL. 133 – TAYLOR SWIFT	00701894 / $16.99
VOL. 135 – MINOR BLUES	00151350 / $17.99
VOL. 136 – GUITAR THEMES	00701922 / $14.99
VOL. 137 – IRISH TUNES	00701966 / $15.99
VOL. 138 – BLUEGRASS CLASSICS	00701967 / $17.99

VOL. 139 – GARY MOORE	00702370 / $17.99
VOL. 140 – MORE STEVIE RAY VAUGHAN	00702396 / $19.99
VOL. 141 – ACOUSTIC HITS	00702401 / $16.99
VOL. 142 – GEORGE HARRISON	00237697 / $17.99
VOL. 143 – SLASH	00702425 / $19.99
VOL. 144 – DJANGO REINHARDT	00702531 / $17.99
VOL. 145 – DEF LEPPARD	00702532 / $19.99
VOL. 146 – ROBERT JOHNSON	00702533 / $16.99
VOL. 147 – SIMON & GARFUNKEL	14041591 / $17.99
VOL. 148 – BOB DYLAN	14041592 / $17.99
VOL. 149 – AC/DC HITS	14041593 / $19.99
VOL. 150 – ZAKK WYLDE	02501717 / $19.99
VOL. 151 – J.S. BACH	02501730 / $16.99
VOL. 152 – JOE BONAMASSA	02501751 / $24.99
VOL. 153 – RED HOT CHILI PEPPERS	00702990 / $22.99
VOL. 155 – ERIC CLAPTON UNPLUGGED	00703085 / $17.99
VOL. 156 – SLAYER	00703770 / $19.99
VOL. 157 – FLEETWOOD MAC	00101382 / $17.99
VOL. 159 – WES MONTGOMERY	00102593 / $22.99
VOL. 160 – T-BONE WALKER	00102641 / $17.99
VOL. 161 – THE EAGLES ACOUSTIC	00102659 / $19.99
VOL. 162 – THE EAGLES HITS	00102667 / $17.99
VOL. 163 – PANTERA	00103036 / $19.99
VOL. 164 – VAN HALEN: 1986-1995	00110270 / $19.99
VOL. 165 – GREEN DAY	00210343 / $17.99
VOL. 166 – MODERN BLUES	00700764 / $16.99
VOL. 167 – DREAM THEATER	00111938 / $24.99
VOL. 168 – KISS	00113421 / $17.99
VOL. 169 – TAYLOR SWIFT	00115982 / $16.99
VOL. 170 – THREE DAYS GRACE	00117337 / $16.99
VOL. 171 – JAMES BROWN	00117420 / $16.99
VOL. 172 – THE DOOBIE BROTHERS	00119670 / $17.99
VOL. 173 – TRANS-SIBERIAN ORCHESTRA	00119907 / $19.99
VOL. 174 – SCORPIONS	00122119 / $19.99
VOL. 175 – MICHAEL SCHENKER	00122127 / $17.99
VOL. 176 – BLUES BREAKERS WITH JOHN MAYALL & ERIC CLAPTON	00122132 / $19.99
VOL. 177 – ALBERT KING	00123271 / $17.99
VOL. 178 – JASON MRAZ	00124165 / $17.99
VOL. 179 – RAMONES	00127073 / $16.99
VOL. 180 – BRUNO MARS	00129706 / $16.99
VOL. 181 – JACK JOHNSON	00129854 / $16.99
VOL. 182 – SOUNDGARDEN	00138161 / $17.99
VOL. 183 – BUDDY GUY	00138240 / $17.99
VOL. 184 – KENNY WAYNE SHEPHERD	00138258 / $17.99
VOL. 185 – JOE SATRIANI	00139457 / $19.99
VOL. 186 – GRATEFUL DEAD	00139459 / $17.99
VOL. 187 – JOHN DENVER	00140839 / $19.99
VOL. 188 – MÖTLEY CRÜE	00141145 / $19.99
VOL. 189 – JOHN MAYER	00144350 / $19.99
VOL. 190 – DEEP PURPLE	00146152 / $19.99
VOL. 191 – PINK FLOYD CLASSICS	00146164 / $17.99
VOL. 192 – JUDAS PRIEST	00151352 / $19.99
VOL. 193 – STEVE VAI	00156028 / $19.99
VOL. 194 – PEARL JAM	00157925 / $17.99
VOL. 195 – METALLICA: 1983-1988	00234291 / $22.99
VOL. 196 – METALLICA: 1991-2016	00234292 / $19.99

Prices, contents, and availability subject to change without notice.

HAL•LEONARD®
www.halleonard.com